Re/Membering

Re/Membering

MEDITATIONS AND SERMONS
FOR THE TABLE OF JESUS CHRIST

Joseph R. Jeter, Jr.

Chalice Press
St. Louis, Missouri

Biblical quotations, unless otherwise noted, are from the *New Revised Standard Version Bible*, copyright 1989, Division of Christian Education of the National Council of the Churches of Christ in the USA. Used by permission. Those quotations marked KJV are from the *King James Version* of the Bible.

Cover design: Lynne Condellone
Art Director: Michael Domínguez

10 9 8 7 6 5 4 3 2 1   96 97 98 99

Library of Congress Cataloging-in-Publication Data

Jeter, Joseph R.
    Re/Membering : meditations and sermons for the Table of Christ / Joseph R. Jeter, Jr.
        p.   cm.
    Includes bibliographical references.
    ISBN 0-8272-3215-2
    1. Lord's Supper—Meditations. 2. Lord's Supper—Sermons.
    3. Sermons, American. I. Title.
BV825.2.J47 1995
242' .2—dc20
                                          95-42788
                                          CIP

Printed in the United States of America

In Memoriam

Joseph R. Jeter, O.D.
Helen V. Jeter

CONTENTS

Introduction

Biblical: THE HEBREW SCRIPTURES

Biblical: THE NEW TESTAMENT

Historical

Literary

Contemporary

INTRODUCTION

Volumes have been written seeking to define the relationship between word and sacrament.[1] This little book simply assumes that this relationship exists and that it is important. It is written because, whatever else may be involved in that relationship, both word and sacrament seek to make God and God's saving work in Christ *present*.[2] It is this making-present that concerns me when we come to what is variously called the Eucharist, the Lord's Supper, holy communion, or simply the sacrament. Unlike baptism, which occurs infrequently enough (alas!) to maintain its power and intensity for us, the frequent observance of the Supper may lead to half-hearted repetition with no sense of presence or power. Whether this common meal of the church, shared in remembrance of Jesus Christ, is repeated daily, weekly, monthly, quarterly or whenever, there is the temptation to rote observance. Yes, there is value in the repetition of the ritual itself, but more so, I suggest, when participants find the sharing of the Supper meaningful. Many church leaders, especially since Luther, have suggested refraining from communion for a time when it has lost its spiritual savor (a kind of sacramental fast).[3] My suggestion is that we struggle through the lack of savor (the Passover meal teaches us the value of bitter herbs) until the taste has been renewed.

This book is concerned with a portion of that relationship between word and sacrament. Sometimes a few words, apart from the words of institution themselves, can be the catalyst that allows the making-present of God to happen. A word, an idea, an image, may strike fire or gently swirl in the hearer's mind, permitting the focus that opens the hearer to God's work in his or her heart.

We are, therefore, not primarily interested here in the words of the liturgy itself, except as they are meditatively interpreted. We are look-

---

[1]See, for example, Dom Gregory Dix's *The Shape of the Liturgy* (London: A & C Black, 1945) and Bernard Cooke's *Ministry to Word and Sacraments* (Philadelphia: Fortress, 1977).

[2]John Macquarrie, *Principles of Christian Theology* (New York: Charles Scribner's Sons, 1966), 387.

[3]See meditation #47.

ing at those "free words" offered in a sermon or meditation prior to the breaking of the bread and the pouring of the cup. What is the relationship between these "free words" and the sacrament? The responses range from crucial to optional. Since Martin Luther believed that the external word of preaching always preceded the internal word given by the Holy Spirit, he went so far as to say the sacrament could not be observed without preaching.[4] Most Protestants have followed him, if not to his extreme position. On the other hand, we find that in some Catholic communities there is often no sermon at the Eucharist. As Peter Moore says, "the apostolic faith flourished without much sermonizing—a fact of which the Reformers took little account."[5] But Catholics are unwilling to give up the importance of the Word, clearly evidenced in Bernard Cooke's affirmation that the Eucharist "is basically an act of proclamation."[6] It is the position of this book that while preaching is not essential to the Lord's Supper, or to any other act of worship for that matter, it is close to being so and can be of great benefit.

What of the separate "communion meditation," as distinct from the sermon or homily? Many believe it to be unnecessary, suggesting that the sermon should "carry" the celebration at the table or, more strongly, that the sermon *is* a communion meditation. I make no judgment on that. I have heard separate meditations that seemed intrusive or irrelevant, that interrupted the movement of the service; I have also heard meditations that were wonderful and greatly added to the experience of communion. One common approach is having a meditation if the celebration of communion precedes the sermon for the day, but not if the sermon comes first in the liturgy. For those who do not use separate meditations for the table, the thoughts and images in this book may perhaps serve as "kindling," in the metaphor of Ian Macpherson,[7] material to help get a sermon on the Supper started.

The meditations and sermons[8] here are offered then to help pastors and worship leaders in the making-present that may occur through this ancient rite of the church. Fifty-two of them (enough for a full year) are drawn from scripture. Another fifty-three-Sunday year's worth comes from history, literature, and seasonal reflections. The remaining thirty-six represent contemporary reflections on eucharistic themes and personal experiences. Some focus specifically upon the action of the Eucharist; others focus upon the relationship between the Eucharist and other affirmations and problems of our faith and life. Some are homely, others more technical. I have felt free to borrow from others' memories,

---

[4]John Dillenberger, *Martin Luther* (Garden City: Doubleday, 1961), xxxi.
[5]Peter C. Moore, *Tomorrow Is Too Late* (London: A. R. Mowbray, 1970), 73.
[6]Cooke, 246.
[7]See Ian Macpherson, *Kindlings* (Old Tappan, NJ: Revell, 1969).
[8]The difference between "meditation" and "sermon" for the purposes of this book is primarily one of length.

since the Supper is larger than any one person's experience of it. Proper credit has in such cases been given, except for those buried so deep in my memory that the source can no longer be found. One may agree or disagree with the images presented, the points made, the conclusions drawn. Disagreement is fertile ground for new ideas. I also make no apologies for the affirmations that are in tension with one another. This table we gather about is a very large one. Is the Eucharist a comfort or a challenge? Well, sometimes it is one, sometimes it is the other, sometimes it is both. Is it a solitary or communal act? Which is more important: the silence or the words? Again, these questions can only be answered for given persons at given moments. All have their place. These one hundred forty-one meditations and sermons have, in all but a few cases, been used in Christian worship. Perhaps they may be of use again.

I express my thanks to Bryan Feille, Betty Curl, Suellen Hartley, and David Polk for their counsel and help. The dedication to my parents, both of whom died this past year, represents a gratitude and a memory stronger than any other in this world for me. Save one. May they rest in peace.

One story before we begin. Edward Lueders was a professor of English at the University of Utah. He had a cabin in the woods near Clam Lake, Wisconsin, that he would retreat to in the summer for writing and respite. In 1970, when he went to open the cabin for his summer stay, he discovered that—while everything was in order—it was not *his* order.[9] Someone had been there. All his food supplies were gone, and in their place was a stack of papers. He began to read, "Dear Professor Lueders: It is obvious that you don't use your cabin in the winter, and it seems well suited to my current needs, so I am going to use your cabin for awhile...."[10] Some months later, his unknown guest wrote:

> My dear Lueders: In a day or two I will leave. I have used your property long enough....The snow still lies deep in your woods. It will be months before you return to the cabin. I have run onto things while I was here, and I have run out of things—like food. Either way, it is time to move on. I am sorry your food has been depleted. It really bothers me to see your supplies getting low and to know I can do nothing about it. I can't pay you back in food....One way or another, though, everything I have used here is a part of what I have written out. I have decided therefore to leave all my writing here when I go.[11]

Lueders later published the writings of his guest under the title *The Clam Lake Papers* (San Francisco: Harper & Row, 1977). He never learned the identity of the person who used his cabin for that winter sabbatical. There are surely those who

---

[9]Edward Lueders, *The Clam Lake Papers* (San Francisco: Harper & Row, 1977), 13.

[10]*Ibid.*, 17.

[11]*Ibid.*, 143.

cannot understand or appreciate an offering of words and thought in gratitude for food received. But I hope the reader is not one of those. For, in essence, that is what you now hold in your hands. I assume that I, like you, have been to the table many times and have been blessed beyond my deserving with the sacramental food of Jesus' suffering and death. I cannot pay for this food, either. So like a pack rat or a winter visitor at Clam Lake, I leave these pages in gratitude and thanksgiving.

Biblical

BIBLICAL:
The Hebrew Scriptures

---

1 FORESHADOWINGS
Genesis 14:18–20

And King Melchizedek of Salem brought out bread and wine; he was priest of God Most High....And Abram gave him one tenth of everything.

The first mention of bread and wine together in the Bible comes during an interlude in the Abram story in Genesis 14 with the mysterious account of Melchizedek. King of Salem and priest of God, Melchizedek came to Abram bringing bread and wine. He blessed Abram, and Abram gave him a tenth of what he had.

This little story has been the subject of much fanciful interpretation within and without scripture. The Book of Hebrews calls Jesus a priest forever after the order of Melchizedek. And the story itself has been seen as a prefigure of the mass.[1] We cannot be sure of this. But there is a curious relationship in this story that remains with us to this day. And that is the relationship between tithing and the elements of bread and wine.

In a number of churches the Lord's Supper directly follows the offering. During the singing of the Doxology the tithes and offerings are brought forward together with the elements of the Supper. The implication—generally unstated—is that these two parts of the liturgy have something to do with each other. As indeed they do. The intimation from the Melchizedek story is absolutely attested in the liturgy of the Lord's Supper. Whatever the order of the service, the offering is a response to the Eucharist. We do not give so that God will give, but because God has given. The priest of God blessed Abram, and Abram responded. God has blessed us beyond measure in the gift of Christ, and we respond with thanksgiving as we receive the symbols of that gift, the bread and wine of this table.

---

[1]The most useful study of the Melchizedek story is that of Fred Horton, *The Melchizedek Tradition* (Cambridge: Cambridge Univ. Press, 1976).

2 ZOAR
Genesis 19:15–23

*"I cannot flee to the hills.... Look, that city is near enough to flee to,
and it is a little one...." Therefore the city was called Zoar.*

I had finished preaching one Sunday years ago in North Canton,
Ohio, and my hosts took me out to eat. We drove out into the country
until we came to a little village by a river. It was called Zoar and there
was a good place to eat. "Zoar...what a strange name," I said. "It is a
Bible name," my host told me. This, of course, would later send me
scurrying first to concordance and then text. What I found there has
lingered in my memory.

The Lot narrative in Genesis 19 is not a particularly appealing one.
God appears both vengeful and gullible. And Lot himself is not a very
admirable character. He is weak, he values courtesy above decency, he
is guilty of drunkenness and incest. But in spite of all that, this nephew
of Abraham is apparently more moral than the wicked Sodomites and
thus worthy of being saved from God's destruction of Sodom and
Gomorrah.

Two angels tell Lot and his family to flee to the hills. But Lot, in his
weakness, protests that he cannot make it that far and suggests the little
city close by as a substitute. The angels agree and postpone the destruction until Lot arrives in the little city of Zoar. Safe in Zoar, they were
commanded not to look back while God rained fire and brimstone upon
Sodom and Gomorrah. Alas, Lot's wife did look back—whether from
curiosity or compassion, we do not know—and was turned into a pillar
of salt.

The little city of Zoar (Zoar means "little") thus entered history as a
synonym for a place of refuge. Time and again it has disappeared from
consciousness only to reappear during times of religious persecution.
For centuries people have left their homes in quest of religious freedom
and called the place of their refuge, figuratively if not literally, Zoar.
And little towns called Zoar are still sprinkled across our maps.

Most of us are fortunate in that we do not face persecution for our
faith. And we are, or should be, grateful. There are, however, two more
things to say about that. First, our situation could change. Second, the
lack of external persecution can often serve to heighten the internal persecution that we face. So many of our lives are a mess. We are laden
with sin and guilt, frustration and depression. In Mr. Spurgeon's words:
"Christ is the only Zoar where we can find refuge from destruction."[2]
Our flight from self-destruction often leads us to the cross and this table.

---

[2]Charles H. Spurgeon, *12 Sermons on the Lord's Supper* (Grand Rapids, MI: Baker
Book House, 1980), 174.

We ask God to hide us behind the cross. We eat this bread and sip this cup to remind us how indebted we are to God for this sanctuary, how grateful we are to Christ for this chance to be born again and born free this time, whatever our external circumstances may be. Come to Zoar. Take refuge if necessary. There is a good place to eat here.

3 WORTHLESS OR SAVORY FOOD?
Genesis 27:1–4; Numbers 21:4–5

"Now then, take your weapons, your quiver and your bow, and go out to the field, and hunt game for me. Then prepare for me savory food, such as I like, and bring it to me to eat, so that I may bless you before I die."

From Mount Hor they set out by the way to the Red Sea, to go around the land of Edom; but the people became impatient on the way. The people spoke against God and against Moses, "Why have you brought us out of Egypt to die in the wilderness? For there is no food and no water, and we detest this miserable food."

Compare these two texts from the Hebrew scriptures. In Genesis 27 old Isaac says to his son Esau, "prepare for me savory food such as I like." In Numbers 21 the children of Israel, on their exodus way, rise up against Moses and whine, "we detest this miserable food."

Two kinds of food: one rich and savory, the other scarce and worthless. And yet, as we all know, the savory food became an instrument of deceit, whereby Jacob tricked Isaac into giving him the blessing intended for Esau. And the worthless food that the Israelites complained about turned out to be the manna sent from God that sustained them in the wilderness.

Alas, rich and savory food can have its reward, as all those who struggle with their waistlines know. And plain, simple food—the manna and oat brans of this world—are, in the long run, not worthless, but valuable for life and health. Griping about food is a national pastime. I have little patience with it and find it unbecoming to people as overfed as we are.

The plain and simple food on this table may not appeal to our palate, but it is far from worthless. Like the manna of God, it can sustain us as we journey through the wilderness of this world, sustain us with a faith in the Christ who loves us, even when we moan and complain. That is a great love. And this is a great meal. Perhaps the most savory meal of all.

4 THE CUPBEARER AND THE BAKER
Genesis 40

Pharaoh was angry with his two officers, the chief cupbearer and the chief baker, and he put them...in the prison where Joseph was confined....They said to him, "We have had dreams, and there is no one to interpret them." And Joseph said to them, "Do not interpretations belong to God? Please tell them to me."

The story in Genesis 40 is remarkable on many levels. Joseph is in prison in Egypt when two of Pharaoh's servants are cast into the dungeon with him: Pharaoh's cupbearer and his baker, the ones who are responsible for his bread and wine. The two have dreams while in prison and Joseph interprets them.[3] In three days the cupbearer will be restored; in three days the baker will be hanged. Joseph's interpretation proves to be correct. After giving him the interpretation, he said to the cupbearer: "Remember me when it is well with you" (v. 14). But the last verse of the story says, "The cupbearer did not remember Joseph, but forgot him" (v. 23).

Consider. Those whose lives revolve around bread and wine are in trouble. One is lost and one is saved. The one who is saved forgets the source of his good news. Our lives, too, revolve around bread and wine. We are responsible for these symbols that Jesus left with us. There is much pain among us; so many, like pharaoh's baker, disappear from the circle. Can we, who have been given the good news of salvation, forget its source? As we eat the bread and drink from the cup, can we forget the one who provided us not only with these symbols, but also with the saving reality behind them? If we are like the cupbearer, who heard good news and then forgot its source, then we keep Jesus in the prison of indifference, far from the center of our lives. There are two ways, then, to lose hope. One is to be rejected. The other—and the one which imperils us—is to forget why we were not rejected.

---

[3]This text would make a remarkable readers' theater or mini-drama for a group in the church.

5 PASSOVER
Exodus 12:13

The blood shall be a sign for you on the houses where you live: when I see the blood, I will pass over you, and no plague shall destroy you when I strike the land of Egypt.

No one has ever doubted that the Lord's Supper is closely related to the Hebrew Passover. Jesus instituted the Supper at a Passover meal. Blood is central to both. And Christians would later say: "Christ our Passover lamb is sacrificed for us" (1 Corinthians 5:7). Jews understood through Passover and Christians through Eucharist that they had been saved—not of their own doing—but by an act of God. There is another similarity between the two rituals less frequently remembered. As Demetrius Dumm tells it, Passover was focused on the Hebrews' call "to tear themselves loose from an attractive and apparent safety in bondage and to embrace instead a journey that was as threatening as it was promising." [4] Roland DeVaux suggests the immediacy of the ritual was even more striking. Rather than simply a remembrance of what God had done in the past, the original ritual prescribed that "those eating it should have their belts already fastened, sandals on their feet (as if they were going to make a long journey on foot), and a shepherd's stick in one hand."[5]

The Eucharist has a similar claim upon Christians. It was designed by Jesus and the church not only to be a ritual where we remember what God has done for us in the past, but also one in which God's claim upon our future is made clear. To partake of the bread and wine is to experience "conversion" once again, to cinch up our belts and put on our shoes, ready for the journey of faith to which we have been called. It is no mistake that in Paul's discussion of the Supper in 1 Corinthians, these verses appear side by side: "Do this, as often as you drink it, in remembrance of me. For as often as you eat this bread and drink the cup, you proclaim the Lord's death until he comes" (11:25b–26). Remember. Then proclaim. Receive. Then respond. Christ our Passover is sacrificed for us. In gratitude let us be about his work.

---

[4]Demetrius Dumm, "Passover and Eucharist," *Worship* 61 (May 1987), 205.
[5]Roland DeVaux, *Ancient Israel: Its Life and Institutions* (New York: McGraw-Hill, 1961), 489. See Dumm, 203.

6 SCAPEGOAT NO LONGER
Leviticus 16:7–10, 20–22

Aaron shall lay both his hands on the head of the live goat, and confess over it all the iniquities of the people of Israel, and all their transgressions, all their sins, putting them on the head of the goat, and sending it away into the wilderness....

One of the early Old Testament images used by the church to describe the person and role of Jesus was that of the scapegoat.[6] Actually, the Day of Atonement ritual involved two goats. One was "for Yahweh" and was slaughtered for the "uncleanness" of the temple. The other was "for Azazel." The sins of the people were confessed on the head of the goat and it was sent alive into the wilderness. Azazel was probably understood in the beginning as a desert demon,[7] but later the "goat for Azazel" was simply excluded, sent away, so that the impurities it bore would no longer corrupt the community.

It is a sad picture—the goat, innocent itself, wandering alone in the desert, with the sins of the people upon its head. One can see why the church would employ this image to speak of what happened to Jesus. The church actually blurred the two goats—one slaughtered, one sent away loaded down with sin—into one image.[8]

I confess that atonement, with its attendant image of scapegoating, has always been difficult for me. The idea that God sent Jesus into the world as we send the scapegoat into the wilderness does not compute. Wondrous love tempered by cruelty? I believe that the crushing of Jesus between state and religion was not God's will, that the crucifixion delayed but did not overcome God's plan for redeeming the world, a plan confirmed in the resurrection. I would rather see Jesus as God's beloved Son than as our scapegoat. He came to be believed, not to be slaughtered. But, when confronted with the sin of the world, Jesus chose to bear the burden of that sin, that we can only accept as a grace beyond our deserving. So, rather than label Jesus a scapegoat who got us off the hook for our actions, I think we should hear the message of this story as one prompting us to action.

What action? This! Let us go into the desert and find the scapegoat, lead it home to its fellow-creatures and good pasture, saying to it what

---

[6] See Romans 5:8; Galatians 3:13; 4:4–5; 1 Peter 2:24.

[7] See *Journal for the Study of Judaism* 18:152-167.

[8] Neither slaughter nor enforced isolation encumbered with sin are attractive alternatives. The cruel childhood tease, "I'd rather be dead than red on the head," begins to point toward the dilemma. In addition, there are those who claim that, by the time of Paul, the scapegoat *was* killed by being pushed off a cliff. See *Studies in Religion* 20:3 (1991), 345-356.

is true: "No longer do we put our sins upon your head; rather, we recognize these sins as our sins and will strive, through the help of God and the witness of Jesus, to do better." Jesus our scapegoat has been exiled to this table. And this is a good place to make our pledge: "Forgive us, Jesus, for blithely dumping our sins on you. But we are not strong enough, and we earnestly ask your help that we might recognize our sinfulness and repent. Grant us God's mercy and God's help, that we might rise above our sins and come closer to what God wants us to be."

7 WORD AND SACRAMENT
Deuteronomy 8:1–3

... one does not live by bread alone, but by every word that comes from the mouth of the LORD.

In the beginning God spoke the world into existence. "And God said...and it was done." Thus from the beginning there has been a close relationship between the words and deeds of God. We recognize this in our worship when we testify to the mutual importance of word and sacrament. The early church, according to Bernard Cooke, arrived at "a radical unification of word and sacrament."[9] As he says:

> This is why...the supreme sacramental expression of the community's faith and life and being is also seen as its supreme prophetic proclamation, "As often as you eat this bread...." (1 Corinthians 11:26).[10]

What we say and do at the table then follows the prior action of God in saying and doing those things necessary for our life and redemption. They go together. A "wordless" Eucharist is impossible. Martin Luther recognized this by requiring that the Eucharist be accompanied by preaching. Nor will a non-eucharistic word, one that ignores the cross, long endure.

More importantly, Jesus recognized it. During his temptation in the wilderness, he is reported to have responded: "One does not live by bread alone, but by every word that comes from the mouth of God" (Matthew 4:4), giving renewed witness to the old affirmation from Deuteronomy about God's provision for our needs. Jesus puts our need for bread in the context of our need for God's word. We come to this table also needing both. And both are present. "On the same night that he was betrayed, he took bread..." is both word and sacrament for a hungry people.

---

[9]Cooke, 230.
[10]*Ibid.*

8 TALITHA, CUMI
Judges 11:29–40; Mark 5:21–23, 35–43

And Jephthah made a vow to the LORD, and said, "If you will give the Ammonites into my hand, then whoever comes out of the doors of my house to meet me, when I return...shall be the LORD'S, to be offered up by me as a burnt offering...." Then Jephthah came to his home at Mizpah; and there was his daughter coming out to meet him with timbrels and with dancing. She was his only child; he had no son or daughter except her....

I am glad that we have gathered about the table today, to break bread and remember. I hope in these remarks to focus upon one aspect of that remembering that has seldom been considered.

Almost thirty years ago I wrote the one great exegesis paper of my life (everybody should write at least one!). It was a study of Judges 11:34–40, and I used what rudimentary skills I had trying to penetrate to the core of the passage. When I got there I found agony and tragedy and horror. And in the thirty years since that time, not a month has gone by in which I have not been haunted by the tragic picture of Jephthah's daughter. Early on, I asked, "What kind of God would allow this to happen?" And then I asked, "What kind of man would do this?" And then I asked, "What kind of people would want this in their scripture?" No answers came; just demons. There were several times that I thought to preach on this text, to exorcise the demons. But I never did, because I had nothing to say.

Two separate events have combined to open *my* mouth today. I read two biographies recently, one of Admiral of the Fleet Lord Louis Mountbatten of Burma, and the other of Joseph Goebbels, propaganda minister of the Third Reich.[11] The books are not important to us today, but both of them contain sections of photographs. In the Mountbatten book there is a photograph of his favorite cousin, the Grand Duchess Marie, daughter of Czar Nicholas II.[12] Marie was something very special, and Mountbatten dreamed of marrying her. In the Goebbels there is a picture of his eldest daughter Helga, described as an intelligent and precocious child.[13]

And yet, on July 16, 1917, Marie, at the age of eighteen, was dragged into a cellar in Ekaterinburg and shot. Why? Because she was the daughter of the czar. That is why. On April 30, 1945, Helga, at the age of thirteen, was dragged kicking and screaming into a cellar of the Fuehrerbunker in Berlin and murdered with an injection of prussic acid. Why? Because

---

[11]Richard Hough, *Mountbatten* (New York: Random House, 1981) and Helmut Heiber, *Goebbels*, tr. John K. Dickinson (New York: Hawthorne, 1972).
[12]Hough, following p. 80.
[13]Heiber, 215, 238.

she was the daughter of Goebbels, and her father was afraid of her falling into the hands of the advancing Allies.[14] I sat the two photographs side by side and stared from one to the other. And it was their eyes! They stared back at me and indicted me and begged me to help and cried out to the world, "I want to live!" As I looked, the photographs of Marie and Helga slowly dissolved into a picture of Jephthah's daughter. And I have to respond. I have to preach about what we have done to our daughters.

It is true that we have not done very well by our sons, either. We have sent them out as fodder to be dazed and deafened by cannon roar. We have believed that if we expose them to enough slaughter to numb their human sensibilities, then if they survive, we will have made them *men*. But there is still a difference. At least we gave them a club or a gun and told them to defend themselves. We just told our daughters to die. We just told them to die.

We live in a time when this is beginning to change, but not nearly fast enough. Scholarship has rediscovered Jephthah's daughter. Phyllis Trible has called upon us to remember and mourn for her:

> The daughter of Jephthah lies slain upon the high places.
> I weep for you, my little sister.
> Very poignant is your story to me;
> > your courage to me is wonderful,
> > surpassing the courage of men.
> How are the powerless fallen,
> > a terrible sacrifice to a faithless vow![15]

But that is not enough. I have lived with her for too long, and wistful memories are not enough. These memories serve to remind me of the archetypal story from the ancient Mediterranean world of the dancing girl brought before the rulers and, for their entertainment, forced to dance until she dies. It is only in Kazantzakis' retelling of that ancient story that I catch a glimpse of the response I need and must have.

After the dancing girl has finally fallen and died, Odysseus comes and gently picks her up, carries her away, and buries her. Then, on her grave, he raises his cry:

> "...O small, small dancer with your supple feet...,
> You served our god and died in his hard service.
> May your ten martial toes be blessed forever and ever....
> O quivering flame that flickered in the desolate air,
> Dear sister, we won't let the ravening earth devour you!
> You'll perch today on palace roofs like a tall flame
> And sweetly sing, a small, small bird with a burning plume,
> You'll come to herald spring like a swift russet swallow."

---

[14]See Hough, 39-40; Heiber, 356.
[15]Phyllis Trible, *Texts of Terror* (Philadelphia: Fortress, 1984), 109.

He stooped, then planted in the ground an almond pit,
So that one day the harbinger of spring might rise,
The almond tree, and in midwinter, armed with flowers,
Drive out the ancient frosthaired nightmare from the ground,
That liberty might braid her hair with scented almond blossoms.[16]

And so, after her three thousand and my forty years, I testify to you that there is no message we can proclaim, no remembrance we can make, and no offering that we can give to Jephthah's daughter that is acceptable...except resurrection!

It has been suggested that Jesus is a type of Isaac, made like Isaac to carry the wood of his own sacrifice up the hill. But I suggest that Jesus is a type of Jephthah's daughter, a small dancer sacrificed to multiple faithless vows. However, like the song says, "They cut me down, but I leapt up high, for I am the dance that will never, never die."[17] The dance of Jesus goes on. Even now we are preparing to share in that dance of new life on Easter morning. So why cannot the dance of Jephthah's daughter be born again? Why cannot the dance that was once used so tragically to celebrate a military victory be resurrected as a joyful dance of peace?

I think our New Testament text shows us the way. The resurrection of Jairus' daughter is one of five passages in the New Testament which preserve the transliterated Aramaic—preserved, in James Sanders' words, as "precious residues" of Jesus and the early church. But the more I look at them, the more I see the whole story writ small in these five expressions:

- to the daughter who was dead, in Mark 5:
  "Talitha cumi" ("Little girl, I say to you, arise.")

- to the man in Mark 7 who could neither hear nor speak:
  "Ephphatha" ("Be opened.")

- to God in Mark 15:
  "Eloi, Eloi, lama sabachthani!" ("My God, my God, why have you forsaken me!)

- from the woman in the garden in John 20:
  "Rabbouni!" ("Master!")

- and from Paul in 1 Corinthians 16:
  "Marana tha." ("Our Lord, come!")

What do we have?

To the woman: "Arise." To the man: "Open your ears and hear. Open your mouth and speak." But did they? Or did they and all the rest for-

---

[16]Nikos Kazantzakis, *The Odyssey: A Modern Sequel*, tr. Kimon Friar (New York: Simon and Schuster, 1958), 233.

[17]From "Lord of the Dance," words by Sydney Carter, 19th cent. Shaker tune adapted by Carter.

sake him, leaving him to cry to the universe, "Why?" Then, when it was over, and too late, the woman finally recognized him and said, "Master." And the apostle pleaded for all of us, "Jesus, come back, we will do better by you next time."

That was the story two thousand years ago. And, except for a few ironic points of sound and light, our men have remained deaf, ears plugged against the sounds of suffering, and silent, tongues cleaved to the roofs of their mouths. Our women have been dehumanized, sent forth to die and stay dead. Will Jesus come back to a deaf and silent and dead world? I do not think so. What would be the point? In the novel called *The Fratricides*, set during the Greek civil war, a priest named Father Yanaros looks out over his warring village on Easter Eve, a village where brother and sister are killing brother and sister, and says with sad conviction, "Christ does not want to be resurrected [here]. He told me so."[18]

Only if our men will hear and speak, *only* if our women will stand up, do we and he and she have a chance. And this is our hope: that remembering is more than just having memories. Remembering, at its best, is a sacred act that approaches the very threshold of resurrection. For example, when we gather about this table, as we are preparing to do today, it is not just we who gather. Rather, again in James Sanders' words:

> In the celebration of the Holy Communion the whole church is present and the barriers of both time and space have been transcended....Wherever and whenever this celebration takes place the church for that moment is the pilgrim church arriving, just about to step over the threshold...surrounded by "so great a cloud of witnesses."[19]

In remembering Jesus about this table, we not only memorialize his death, we long for his resurrection. And this remembrance and this hope give new life to the whole church, to all the saints. Christ comes to live in us, and through him that great cloud of witnesses comes to us and encounters us and calls us to accountability.

The Mark passage goes even one step farther. *"Talitha, cumi!"* Resurrection in this scene moves subtly out of the province of hope and into the category of commandment. Jesus did not say, "Little girl, I hope you get up." He said, "Get up."

And I choose to take that commandment as universal. Jesus was and is in the "getting-up" business, and as his servants, so must we be. Simply calling to mind and then forgetting Jephthah's daughter and the myriads of others who were cut down before they could flower as persons is no better than calling Jesus to mind and then forgetting him. The

---

[18]Kazantzakis, *The Fratricides*, tr. Athena Gianakas Dallas (New York: Simon and Schuster, 1964), 160.

[19]James A. Sanders, "In the Same Night," *God Has a Story, Too* (Philadelphia: Fortress, 1979), 96.

true remembrance is the one with staying power.

Therefore on this day I claim in Christ my portion of the enduring life and work and dance of Jephthah's daughter. And I put your portion of that burden and that possibility upon you that, as Christ lives in us and we in Christ, so she, through us, might live and dance again.

We are going to "get up" and come forward to receive communion today: in memory of Jesus, in anticipation of the Christ who comes again, and in honor of his resurrection message to the world. And as we come, I offer these words of memory and commitment:

"Little sister, I do not even know your name, but out of your dust blowing in the wind of the Judean desert, I claim your dance. And I call upon your sisters here to rise up and claim their own lives of faith, their own right to walk the jubilee road, their own chance to dance beneath the diamond sky with one hand waving free, their own power to rise up and tear down the bars that surround this table and this pulpit in so many places and under so many systems even to this day."

A few weeks ago one of you asked me about a certain seminary. I knew nothing about it, so I went to the library to look at their catalogue. I naturally turned to the field of homiletics. Here is the description of their basic preaching course: "The theory and practice of preaching. Students will prepare, present, and evaluate sermons. Individual attention and evaluation will be provided. For men only."

I would dearly love for this to be the last generation that ever has to put up with that. It is time for the sisters of Jephthah's daughter to minister from the table, to distribute the sacraments of grace and mercy and peace to all of God's children. It is time for her sisters to climb into the pulpit to speak a good word for Jesus Christ. And do not be discouraged as you do. Do not be discouraged by ignorance and intransigence or even by goodhearted people who try but so often say the wrong thing.

Therefore, little boy, beloved man, dear brother, I say to you, "Be opened." Open your ears to the rhythms of your own heart, to the lovely murmurs of the seasons, to the cries of those who suffer and die. And open your mouth. Not to utter faithless vows, but to speak courage to the living and comfort for the dying, to replace the noise of solemn assemblies with a song of the soul. Open your ears and open your mouth and open the road that leads toward tomorrow. There are so many of us and we are such a lonely crowd. Separately, single-file, we will never make it. And Jesus will never come back. But side by side with our sisters, we have a chance.

Little girl, beloved woman, dear sister, I say to you, "Arise." Get up and get on the road. Drive the ancient frosthaired nightmare out of the ground. Lead us out of this winter of our discontent and into the springtime of faith. I say to you, arise, for the long dark night is over, and it is time for the almond tree to bloom.

Marana tha!

9 COMMON BREAD IS HOLY BREAD
1 Samuel 21:1–6

*"Give me five loaves of bread, or whatever is here." The priest
answered David, "I have no ordinary bread at hand, only holy
bread...."*

In 1 Samuel 21, David is on the run from Saul, who seeks to kill
him. He comes to the priestly center at Nob and asks Ahimelech the
priest for bread. David is hungry. The priest, however, has no common
bread, only holy bread, the Bread of the Presence, kept on the altar before Yahweh. David is desperate and deceives the priest, telling him that
he is on an important mission for the king. The priest finally yields and
gives the bread to David.[20] What I ask you to engage in this text is that
the sacred substance, in this case the Bread of the Presence, was used
for secular purposes, the feeding, as the priest thought, of soldiers—in
actuality, a fugitive.

At the Last Supper of Jesus with his disciples, this process was reversed. Jesus took common bread, blessed it, and used it for a holy purpose. This contrast demonstrates that holiness does not reside in substance, but rather in intention and action. Jesus said, "You are my friends
if you do what I command you" (John 15:14). This common meal becomes holy when we eat it in remembrance of him. Our common lives
become holy when we live them according to his commandments. Are
we wretched sinners or the beloved friends of Jesus? The answer to that
questions lies in the answers to these two questions. What is on this
plate? Common bread or the body of Christ? Is this cup filled with grape
juice or the blood of Christ? You tell me. Come.

---

[20]Later on, Ahimelech and all the priests at Nob, save one, are murdered by Saul
for their complicity with David (but that is another story); as is the fact that the bread
was obtained by duplicitous means; as is the fact that the remarks about women in this
text are stereotypical and offensive.

10 MAKE ME A LITTLE CAKE
1 Kings 17:8–16

"Do not be afraid; go and do as you have said; but first make me a little cake...."

The stories surrounding the prophet Elijah are among the most fascinating in all of scripture and repeatedly witness to the power of God. One of these stories concerns Elijah's foray to Zarephath, deep in Baal country. There the prophet, hungry and thirsty, encounters a poor widow and the following dialogue takes place:

> "Bring me a little water." And as she was going to bring it, he called to her and said, "Bring me a morsel of bread in your hand."
>
> "As the LORD your God lives, I have nothing...only a handful of meal, a little oil and two sticks, to prepare it for myself and my son, that we may eat it and die."
>
> "Fear not; go and do as you have said; but first make me a little cake and bring it to me" (17:10–13).

The widow risks her life in doing so, and is rewarded with her meal and oil being sustained, a miracle in which the meal and oil prefigure the loaves and fish of the feeding of the five thousand.

One of the remarkable things about this story is the minimalist language (a little water, a morsel of bread, a handful of meal, a little oil, two sticks, a little cake).[21] Here in Baal country, where Baal, the god of abundant rain and good crops, has failed, Elijah shows how the power of God can be demonstrated through these very little things.

These little things on the table before us—a bit of bread, a sip of wine—are in their own way examples of the awesome power of God. "Jesus, who did not count equality with God a thing to be exploited, emptied himself and took the form of a servant.... He humbled himself and became obedient unto death—even death on a cross" (Philippians 2:7). As we eat and drink, we are confronted with the fact that this same slain lamb, crushed by the power of this world, is now Lord of the universe. Take a morsel of bread, remember that, and give thanks.

---

[21]See Richard D. Nelson, "God and the Heroic Prophet: Preaching the Stories of Elijah and Elisha," in *Quarterly Review* 9:2 (Summer, 1989), 97.

11 GLORY TO GOD AND FOOD FOR PEOPLE
2 Chronicles 6:41—7:5

"Now rise up, O LORD God, and go to your resting place, you and the ark of your might...." When Solomon had ended his prayer, fire came down from heaven and consumed the burnt offering and the sacrifices; and the glory of the LORD filled the temple....King Solomon offered as a sacrifice twenty-two thousand oxen and one hundred twenty thousand sheep....

I was talking with a Bible scholar about a text when he smiled and said, "You spend too much time in Genesis. You need to spend some time in Chronicles." The only thing he did wrong in that exchange was to smile. Because Chronicles is tough. Take the story of the dedication of the temple in 2 Chronicles 6 and 7. It is not unlike church building dedications we have today. There are speeches and prayers and a barbecue. It is just the immensity of it that floors me. Solomon offered up 22,000 oxen and 120,000 sheep as dedicatory sacrifices to God! Can you imagine?

I thought, "Do we really think God wants or needs that kind of sacrifice? Must 142,000 animals be slaughtered to show God how religious we are?" Well, of course not. But we need to understand the nature of biblical sacrifice. After the animals were symbolically offered to God, the meat became food for people, especially the poor. And this sacrifice, the largest I know of in scripture, would have fed a good portion of the whole country. The dedication of the temple was then followed by a feast of gigantic proportions. Glory was given to God and hungry people all over the land were fed.

It is an amazing story and still a little hard for me to swallow. As is the cross. The sacrifice of Christ is one of huge proportions. God is glorified and hungry people all over the world are fed, even to this day, even to this table. It is too large for me. I shy away from the immensity of it. But there it is. Glory to God. And food for people.

12 TOO BAD TO COME TO THE TABLE?
2 Chronicles 33:1–20

Manasseh was twelve years old when he began to reign; he reigned fifty-five years in Jerusalem. He did what was evil in the sight of the LORD....[Then] he prayed to him, and God received his entreaty and heard his plea....

Once, in 1985, a good preacher named Bruce Swett began a sermon by setting two stories side by side. Here, in summary form, is what he said.

The end was near. In January the Russian army had overrun Poland, the Western front was falling apart, there was dissention among his generals. But he still had hope. Then Berlin itself was surrounded and his people fled in the face of the Russian advance. He was living in a bunker in the Reich Chancellery. On the radio he heard that his ally Mussolini had been killed, his body hung upside down outside of a garage in Milan. He decided then that he would not be treated that way. When it was his time to die, he would end his life and have his corpse burned.

On April 28 (eight days after his birthday), the Russians neared the bunker—the fighting was only a few hundred yards away. About midnight, on a spur-of-the-moment decision, he decided to marry his companion, Eva Braun. The next day, April 29, 1945, he said good-bye to his staff, and went to his quarters with Eva. As they had planned, she bit into a poison capsule and lay on the floor. He put a pistol to his head.

What was going through Adolf Hitler's mind at that point? And what if, just before he pulled the trigger, in a moment of exceptional clarity and lucidity, he saw all that he had done, and knew for the first time that it was evil before God?

What if Hitler saw this, and repented, praying to God for forgiveness? WOULD GOD HAVE FORGIVEN HIM?

How could God forgive someone who had caused as much evil and suffering as Adolph Hitler? It seems inconceivable.

This is not, however, an imaginary "what if" game—it actually happened!

Manasseh was the son of good King Hezekiah, and he was the worst king in the history of the Jewish people. He was a vassal to the Assyrians, undid Hezekiah's reforms, set up the worship of other gods, desecrated the temple, put up idols, encouraged abominations, sacrificed his own sons, and persecuted God's prophets. It was Manasseh's sins that caused the Jews to be sent into the dispersion and torment of the Babylonian exile. He reigned for fifty-five years. And he destroyed the Jewish people.

AND YET! God forgave Manasseh and brought him back to Jerusalem!

*"While he was in distress he entreated the favor of the LORD his God and humbled himself greatly before the God of his ancestors. He prayed to him, **and God received his entreaty, heard his plea, and restored him again to Jerusalem and to his kingdom**" (2 Chronicles 33:12–13).*

That must have been some prayer![22]

---

[22]Based on a sermon by Bruce Swett, "Our God Is Not Fair," in HOWO 7750, Advanced Preaching Workshop, Brite Divinity School, Fort Worth, TX, Fall, 1985. Used with permission.

Yea, verily. The fascinating contrast that Swett sets before us demonstrates a number of things. Among them, of course, is the always surprising news that God's ways are not our ways. Rather than ask stuffily, "How can God do that?" perhaps we might remember that the fact God can bring good out of evil means there is hope for us.

At the table we recall again how God brought good (salvation) out of evil (the crucifixion). And rather than wonder how God did that, it is better for us to remember gratefully that because God did, there is hope for us as well.

(See also Meditation #47.)

13 THE ANTIDOTE
Nehemiah 1:11b—2:1a

At that time, I was cupbearer to the king…when wine was served him, I carried the wine and gave it to the king.

Before he went to Jerusalem, Nehemiah served as a cupbearer to the king. His job was to taste the wine before it was served to the king. If the wine was poisoned and the cupbearer died, then the king would not drink it. It was, as one might expect, a position of great honor and trust. And it was through that relationship of trust that Nehemiah received permission to rebuild Jerusalem.

To use the same symbol, Jesus served as cupbearer to the whole human race. He drank the bitter cup for us, drank it to the bottom. And it was poisoned, poisoned with our sin. And he did die. But before he died, as a sort of last will and testament, he did a strange thing. He gave the cup to us and asked us to drink it. That puts us in a real bind. We know it is poisoned, but we drink it every time we gather about this table—we come in fear and trembling for our very lives—and then we find that because he drank it first, all the poison is gone, the sin is forgiven, and it is the sweetest drink we have ever had.

All honor and trust then be to Jesus Christ, who labors with us now to build the new Jerusalem. Eat, drink, give thanks, build!

14 DRINK, DRINK, DRINK
Psalm 75:8

For in the hand of the LORD there is a cup with foaming wine, well mixed; he will pour a draught from it, and all the wicked of the earth shall drain it down to the dregs.

This is a strange text that speaks of a strange cup. No cup of blessing, this. It is a cup of anguish and wrath. Two images emerge. The first is the paradox of the wrathful cup. In a New Testament parallel Jesus drank of the cup of suffering, offering us before he died the cup of blessing. The paradox carries over to this table. With this cup we drink the cup to the dregs, asking for forgiveness and new life. We drink in sadness and in joy because, as the old hymn says, on Calvary, "sorrow and love flow mingled down."

The second image is quantitative. At first glance foaming wine, well mixed, probably with sweet spices and pomegranates, sounds like a good thing. But here it is not to be sipped and enjoyed; rather, the huge cup is poured forcibly down the throats of the wicked, gagging swallow after swallow. Drinking it is no pleasure, but a horrible punishment. The image is similar to that of Numbers 11 where the people cry and plead and pester God for meat, until finally God says, "You want meat? I will give you meat…until it comes out your nostrils and becomes loathesome to you."

Once, after a couple of years in Africa, I was driving down a road and saw something I had not seen since leaving America: pigs. Most people in that area were Muslims who did not eat pork. But this Lebanese farmer raised pigs. I stopped and asked if there was any pork available. He said yes, that he would send some to our house. And send it he did. Over a hundred pounds of pork. We had no refrigerator and, fearing trichinosis if the meat spoiled, several of us set out to eat as much as we could immediately. Within a day we did not care if we saw no pork for two more years. Too much of anything loses its appeal.

A force-fed gospel is no longer worthy of its name: good news. This is why we are invited to faith and discipleship, invited to this table. Come, if you will, to partake of these symbols of sorrow and love. Come, if you will, to partake of just enough bread and wine to help you meditate on Christ's suffering and our redemption. Come, if you will, not to gorge and gag and be satiated, but to be renewed by the bread of the presence and the cup of blessing.

15 EATING THE BREAD OF ANXIOUS TOIL
Psalm 127:1–2

It is in vain that you rise up early and go late to rest, eating the bread
of anxious toil....

"Eating the bread of anxious toil." Is there anyone here who can identify with that? I surely can. Joe Roos has written:

> Busyness has become a way of life for many of us, even a status symbol. Our work is justified only if we are continually active and preoccupied. There are so many necessary and urgent things to be done. After one task is completed, there are others always waiting in the wings, needing our immediate attention. To slow down, to rest, often seems out of the question, a lack of commitment, a sign of weakness. Not only our days, but many of our weekends become filled too. We are not just eating the bread of anxious toil; we are daily gulping down loaf after loaf after loaf. "Give us this day," we pray, "our daily bread (of anxious toil)."[23]

I had a student last year who had transferred from Cal Tech. He could not take it any more. He told me that the day he knew he was finished there, he had sat down to eat with several other students. They pushed their food around disinterestedly until finally one of them said, "This eating is a waste of time; I could be studying." And he rushed off to his room to eat some more bread of anxious toil.

This, friends, is not the bread of anxious toil. This is a different kind of bread. As we eat it together, peacefully, quietly, and among friends, as we think on the past and the future, we can yield up the moment to God and rest in God's presence. This little service, shared beneath the cross of Jesus, can be for us "a home within the wilderness, a rest upon the way, from the burning of the noontide heat and the burden of the day."[24]

---

[23]Joe Roos, "Eating the Bread of Anxious Toil," *Sojourners* 11:6 (June 1982), 3.
[24]"Beneath the Cross of Jesus," words: Elizabeth C. Clephane, music: Frederick C. Maker.

16 AT TABLE, ONE
Psalm 133

How very good and pleasant it is when kindred live together in unity!

A friend was speaking about a powerful moment in his first pastor-ate back during the Vietnam War. He had been a dove on the war issue, and he had a member, who worked for an armaments plant, who was an unabashed hawk. They could not have been farther apart, and the ten-sion between them was great. My friend preached on occasion about the war, and this member always spoke against him when he did. He even tried to have the pastor fired. One day the congregation altered their usual pattern and came forward to receive communion. First in line was the member I have mentioned. He approached the pastor and, as the elements were being handed to him, their eyes met—and stayed locked. The man began to cry. So did the pastor. He set down the paten and chalice and embraced the man there at the table. No words needed to be said or were. Their respective positions on the war did not change, but their relationship did. In an instant at the table.

This is a fascinating text. "How very good it is when kindred live together in unity! It is like the precious oil on the head, running down upon the beard, on the beard of Aaron." Here the psalmist reflects upon the joys of fraternal harmony, comparing it to the ordination of Aaron as priest of the people. This ordination is found in Leviticus 8, which I offer as perhaps the grisliest chapter in the Bible. Every detail of the slaughter of animals used to celebrate this ordination is given. If we ordained ministers that way today, no one would be ordained. I know it is from another time, but I find the text repugnant. A better name for the chapter would be "Slaughterhouse 8." And the distance between my dis-gust at this event and the psalmist's celebration of it seems too great to bridge. "How wonderful it is when we live in unity, with the blood and oil dripping down our beards." Right.

But it is just this distance bridged by the blood of the cross. Strange but true. A cruel death brings us together. Symbols of that amazing bridge are here before us on the table. My friend and his former "enemy" met there and were transformed. We can be, too. You do not need to get up physically right now, but I do invite you to consider in your hearts if there is someone with whom you are in trouble: in your family, in this fellowship, wherever. In your heart invite that person to come to the table with you and partake together. Follow this experience with prayer for reconciliation. It may be the starting place for new life between you and that person. The table of Jesus Christ is the longest in the world—it reaches around the earth—and also the shortest, reaching from you to your neighbor. "How very good and pleasant it is when kindred live together in unity."

17 WISDOM'S WAY
Proverbs 9:1–6

Wisdom has built her house,…she has also set her table. She has sent out her servant girls, she calls from the highest places in the town, "You that are simple, turn in here!" To those without sense she says, "Come, eat of my bread and drink of the wine that I have mixed. Lay aside immaturity, and live, and walk in the way of insight."

One of the expressions for divine personality used in scripture is Wisdom. In Proverbs 9 "Woman Wisdom" invites the unwise or simple to a banquet, as opposed to "Dame Folly," who later invites them to partake of her stolen water.[25] This is slightly different from other affirmations we see about the beauty of simplicity, about how it is better to be simple than wise. It is rather an affirmation of vulnerability and grace. The poor, the unwise, the simple are often ignored, marginalized or victimized in our world. But God loves them dearly and has prepared a special banquet for them.

This reminds us, or should, that all our "wisdom" is folly before God, that we who think ourselves so wise, so in control, in truth know very little. Christ crucified is offensive to us. And this little meal of remembrance sometimes offends us by its very simplicity. Can anything this simple be really important? Yes, it can. It is important *and* it is dangerous. Isaiah points out the danger of vain worship: "When you stretch out your hands, I will hide my eyes from you; even though you make many prayers, I will not listen" (1:15). The invitation, which goes out to all, calls us to come humbly to Wisdom's banquet and know that the holy is in our midst. This table is a dear gift to the unwise. And we who know-it-all need that gift most desperately.

---

[25]Adapted from notes to Proverbs 9 in the *New Oxford Annotated Bible* (New York: Oxford Univ. Press, 1991), 812.

18 THE APPLE TREE
Song of Solomon 2:3

As an apple tree among the trees of the wood, so is my beloved among young men.

"To discuss the significance of the Eucharist in a Jewish framework is an extremely delicate task...."[26] With these words Eric Werner introduces his comments on the Eucharist. One might expect no Jewish view of the Eucharist at all. But such is not the case. One example is found in an early Midrash on Psalm 34:8: "Taste and see that the LORD is good," where the word "Chrestos" is found. In another sixth-century Midrash, *Exodus Rabba*, are found these comments on Exodus 12:22: "Take a bunch of hyssop, dip it in the blood...and touch the lintel and the two doorposts with the blood in the basin":

> Another interpretation...it is written: *"As an apple tree among the trees of the wood, so is my beloved among young men"* (Song of Solomon 2:3). Why is God compared to an apple tree? To teach you that just as the apple though unattractive yet possesses good taste and flavour, so the Holy One, blessed be He; *"His speech is most sweet, and he is altogether desirable"* (5:16). He appeared to the heathens, yet they would not accept the Torah, which was in their eyes a thing of no value. God has taste and fragrance...for it says: *"O Taste and see that the LORD is good...."*

> There are many other things which appear lowly, yet with which God commanded many precepts to be performed. The hyssop, for instance, appears to [people] to be of no worth, yet its power is great in the eyes of God....He performed miracles with the smallest things, and through the hyssop which is the most lowly of trees, did He redeem Israel. Hence is He like *"An apple tree among the trees of the wood."*[27]

Hypothetically at least, according to Werner, this may be seen as an allusion to Christ, with the crucifixion understood as analogous to the Exodus, where the sprinkled blood of the lamb (by the hyssop) saved the Israelites. Thus the Midrash reveals:

> ... an attitude toward Christ and Christianity at the same time belittling and respecting it—belittling it by comparing Christ with the blood-sprinkling hyssop, respecting it by considering Christ an instrument to save Israel.[28]

This is quite interesting. Not only does it offer an opportunity for Jewish-Christian dialogue, it makes a fascinating point about the Eu-

---

[26]Eric Werner, "The Eucharist in Hebrew Literature during the Apostolic and Post-Apostolic Epoch," in *The Eucharist in Ecumenical Dialogue*, ed. Leonard Swidler (New York: Paulist, 1976), 126.

[27]*Ibid.,* 128-129.

[28]*Ibid.,* 130.

charist itself. Seeing Jesus as bread and wine or hyssop or an apple tree does **be-little** him. It reduces him to less than he was, but at the same time offers wide opportunities for understanding and interpreting in the same way as does the Revelation image of the "slain lamb."

Somehow the metaphor of Jesus Christ as apple tree entered Christian consciousness of the Eucharist and stayed. Lowly but delicious. One lovely example is the Scottish folk song, here reproduced from the arrangement by K. Lee Scott:

> The tree of life my soul hath seen,
> Laden with fruit and always green:
> The trees of nature fruitless be
> Compared with Christ, the apple tree.
>
> Christ's beauty doth all things excell:
> By faith I know but ne'er can tell
> The glory which I now can see
> In Jesus Christ, the apple tree.
>
> For happiness I long have sought,
> And pleasure dearly I have bought:
> I missed of all; but now I see
> 'Tis found in Christ, the apple tree.
>
> I'm weary with my former toil,
> Here I will sit and rest awhile:
> Under the shadow I will be,
> Of Jesus Christ, the apple tree.
>
> This fruit doth make my soul to thrive,
> It keeps my dying faith alive;
> Which makes my soul in haste to be
> With Jesus Christ, the apple tree.[29]

Come now to the table. Taste and see that the Lord is good!

---

[29]"The Apple Tree," Scottish folk song, arranged by K. Lee Scott (Chapel Hill: Hinshaw Music, 1983).

19 THE SPICED WINE OF THE POMEGRANATE
Song of Solomon 8:2

I would lead you and bring you into the house of my mother, and into the chamber of the one who bore me. I would give you spiced wine to drink, the juice of my pomegranates.

Charles H. Spurgeon (1834–1892) was one of the greatest preachers in Christian history. When he preached in the Metropolitan Tabernacle in London, his listeners "wept one minute and laughed the next."[30] He was known for his "thoroughly biblical expository sermons."[31] And I have often read them to my profit. Imagine my surprise then, when I chanced upon a sermon called "The Spiced Wine of the Pomegranate."[32] The text given is Song of Solomon 8:2. Somewhat familiar with imagery from the song, I began to read, curious about what he would do with this text for a communion sermon. Imagine my greater surprise when he never mentioned the text in his sermon. Not once! The reading of the text was apparently the last his listeners would hear of it.

Actually, I am not all that surprised. Once we stopped allegorizing the song to death, we accepted it for what it was: beautiful erotic love poetry (and none more suggestive than the section where Spurgeon's text is found). I suspect this is a case, as Eugene Lowry puts it, of "superficial connections."[33] Spurgeon saw the pretty phrase "spiced wine of the pomegranate," remembered the pomegranate as an old symbol for the resurrected Christ, put that together with wine, and began thinking about communion. Worse preachers than Spurgeon have treated texts that way. As Lowry warns: "... forcing Old Testament passages to undergird or embellish the gospel lesson, when they have other agenda, is neither good theology nor good biblical exegesis."[34] Spurgeon clearly had no idea what this text was about. He did at least have the wisdom to omit it from the sermon itself.

The point I am after is this: Scripture is layered with meaning; no one interpretation exhausts a text. However, it is best not to stray too far from the original intention of the text, as best we can determine it. And we may abuse the Hebrew Scriptures by a too easy shift into New Testament language. Spurgeon might have intended "the spiced wine of the pomegranate" as a felicitous reminder of the Last Supper. But before we let the aroma of spiced wine lure us to languor, remember that the only spice in the cup Jesus was given to drink was vinegar. Come carefully to this table now. No romantic idylls, no spiced wine here. Just suffering and salvation.

---

[30]Ian Maclaren, *Beside the Bonnie Brier Bush* (New York: Hurst & Co., n.d.), 60.
[31]Spurgeon, *12 Sermons. . . .*, cover.
[32]*Ibid.,* 159ff.
[33]Eugene Lowry, *Living with the Lectionary* (Nashville: Abingdon, 1992), 20-21.
[34]*Ibid.,* 21.

20 REMEMBER...THEN FORGET
Isaiah 43:18–19; 46:8–11

"Do not remember the former things, or consider the things of old....Remember the former things of old."

One model for biblical studies suggests that we find meaning not only in the affirmations of texts, but also in the tensions within and between texts. For example, in the book of Isaiah there are two interesting commandments just three chapters apart. In chapter 43 God says, "Do not remember the former things, or consider the things of old. I am about to do a new thing...." In chapter 46 God says, "... remember former things of old...I have planned, and I will do it."[35]

Standing these two passages up next to one another makes it sound like God has the same problem with remembering and forgetting that we do. Are we to remember...or not? The answer, while not satisfactory to those who want easy solutions, has to be: some things you must remember; some things you must forget.

Second Isaiah calls upon Israel to forget the suffering of the Exile, because God is about to do something so wonderful that past troubles will pale in comparison. But Israel must not forget the eternal promises of God, because those promises are solid and will be fulfilled.

Just as there is a sense in which choosing means rejecting (to choose a Ford is to reject a Chevy), there is also a sense in which remembering means forgetting (to remember Christ at the Lord's Table is to forget our alienation from Christ, to put it behind us so that we may live in closer communion with the Eternal Now).

We are often reminded at the table about those things we should remember. The other side of that is also important and is witnessed by the apostle Paul: "Forgetting what lies behind and straining forward to what lies ahead, I press on toward the goal for the prize of the heavenly call of God in Christ Jesus" (Philippians 3:13–14).

---

[35] I am indebted to my friend Bryan Feille for pointing out this interesting parallel.

21 HO!
Isaiah 55:1–2

Ho, everyone who thirsts, come to the waters; and you that have no money, come, buy and eat!

A sermon by James Forbes introduced me to the wonder of this little text.[36] How marvelous for those living in poverty to hear the words, "You that have no money, come, buy and eat." Note the text does not say, "You that have no money, come and eat." No, you have to buy your spiritual food. It is not free. It costs. But it does not cost money. It costs something else. Belief. Repentance. Righteousness. And so, this amazing good news, that all of God's goodness is available to you, comes with the proviso that what you have also belongs to God.

Because this ancient intimation of the cost of discipleship was likely to be missed by those mired in their own lethargy, the prophet began with a shout to get their attention: *Ho!* We do not shout much anymore in church. Is it because there is nothing that we really want to call to people's attention? Or is it because the faith we proclaim is too easy and requires little attention or effort? Is nobody thirsty or hungry for the gifts of God? Or are we just afraid of the cost? The psalmist tells us that "God has gone up with a shout" (Psalm 47:5). Perhaps this quietest of all moments of worship needs an occasional attention-getting shout as well. "Ho, everyone who thirsts, come to the waters; and you that have no money, come, buy and eat!"

---

[36]"Ho!" A sermon by James Forbes at the annual meeting of the Academy of Homiletics, Princeton, NJ, 5 Dec. 1990.

22 TELL US SOMETHING WE DON'T ALREADY KNOW! Jeremiah 13:12–14

*"You shall speak to them this word: 'Thus says the L*ORD*, the God of Israel, "Every wine-jar should be filled with wine."' And they will say to you, 'Do you think we do not know that every wine-jar should be filled with wine?'"*

Jeremiah faced the preacher's dilemma—his people thought they knew it all. When he offered them God's word, they received it with a snickering putdown: "We know that. Tell us something we don't already know!" But did they really know it?

We come to the table of the Lord all the time. We know what we are doing here. Or at least we think we do. Then comes an image, a word, a feeling—and the Spirit breaks upon us anew and it is as if we are here for the very first time.

For example, I was sitting quietly at a communion service once when the preacher said, in the course of her remarks, that "the opposite of remember is not forget; the opposite of remember is dismember."[37] I was stunned. I had never thought of that before. Similarly, I remember the time years ago when I was in worship in a Roman Catholic church. When it was time to come forward to receive the Eucharist, the priest invited all of us, Catholic and non-Catholic, to come forward. We were surprised at the invitation, but many of us went forward and knelt at the rail. I put out my hands as I saw others do and, when the priest came to me, I looked up at him. I saw the sweat pouring from his face and realized the risk he had taken to invite me there. At that moment the risk of Jesus and of our faith came clear in a way it had not done before. How many have risked how much that we might receive the blessings of God?

Well, here we are again. Same old words. Same old stuff on the table. We know all about this. Be quick about it. But maybe not too quick. Things can happen here. Things like peace and love and understanding…and salvation. Sometimes we need clever interpretations. But sometimes we need the word that came to Jeremiah's know-it-all people: "Thus says the LORD!"

I think I will shut up now. Come, all who will, to the table.

---

[37]Rita Nakashima Brock, sermon preached at St. Luke's United Church of Christ, Jeffersonville, IN, 18 Oct. 1987. See meditation #106.

23 EZEKIEL BREAD
Ezekiel 4:9–10

"And you, take wheat and barley, beans and lentils, millet and spelt; put them into one vessel, and make bread for yourself."

We had friends over for dinner. After dessert and coffee, we sat and, naturally, talked about dieting. Many are the diets that people have tried in the quest to lose weight. As they were discussed, I decided I was partial to the grapefruit and banana diets, because at least I liked fruit. Then a friend stumped us when she mentioned a diet her mother had tried. It consisted of eating nothing but "Ezekiel bread." No one had heard of it. The assertion that it was both biblical and effective sent us scurrying for our Bibles.

Here is the scene. Ezekiel, exiled in Babylon, is engaged in a kind of prophetic theater in which he mimics the siege of Jerusalem. The prophet is commanded to prepare siege rations. Since no one grain is present in sufficient quantity to make bread, a number of grains are combined, yielding a bread that was nourishing if not particularly tasty.[38]

There can be two explanations for the command to eat this unusual bread, and both of them are interesting. First, the ingredients were available. If you do not have what you want, make use of what you have— just as Jesus did with the water at Cana, the loaves and fishes by the Sea of Galilee, the bread and wine in the upper room. Second, even if other things were available, these were the ingredients that the prophet, and by extension, the people, needed. These ingredients contained the nutrients necessary to save and preserve the people—just as the sacrifice of Jesus, represented in these emblems of his body and blood, contains what is necessary to save us.

I do not know whether or not eating Ezekiel bread will help you lose weight, and I cannot speak for the pedigree of the bread which is before us. But I do know that partaking of this bread and cup is a witness to the gaining of salvation. It may not be tasty, but it is what we have. And it is just what we need.

---

[38]See Moshe Greenberg, *Ezekiel 1–20* (Garden City: Doubleday, 1983), 106, and Joseph Blenkinsopp, *Ezekiel* (Louisville: John Knox, 1990), 34-38.

24 LAMENTATION AND HOPE
Lamentations 1:7–12; 2:11–12; 3:19–24

Jerusalem remembers, in the days of her affliction and wandering....
All her people groan as they search for bread;...babes faint in the
streets of the city. They cry to their mothers, "Where is bread and
wine?"

One of the realities which tugs at the edges of our communion service is the fact that we are eating while much of the world is hungry. I have often wondered what it would be like to be a priest or pastor in a famine-stricken area. Could one serve the Eucharist without people attacking the table for the bread and wine? And if the people restrained themselves, how would one portion out the elements: more to the starving, less to those in better condition? We delude ourselves if we think this feast can be celebrated in ignorance of world hunger.

Jeremiah's poignant lamentations tell the story of a once-great city laid waste and beset with hunger, a proud people reduced to begging for food. The texts contain three elements—the eloquent voice of grief: "Is there any sorrow like my sorrow?" (1:12); the confession of sin: "Jerusalem sinned grievously, so she has become a mockery (1:8);" and the expression of hope: "The steadfast love of the Lord never ceases, his mercies never come to an end; they are new every morning; great is your faithfulness. 'The Lord is my portion,' says my soul, 'therefore I will hope in him'" (3:22–24).

Jeremiah's prescription is a good one for remembering as we come to the table in a starving world. We can bring our grief to God that so many of the people that Jesus died to save are denied the basic necessities of life. We can confess our sins of consumerism that exacerbate the problem. And we can affirm our hope in Christ that with God's grace and compassionate, intelligent policies of sharing, the suffering may be assuaged.

BIBLICAL:
The New Testament

---

25 TELL THEM WILLIE BOY WAS HERE
Matthew 2:16–18

When Herod saw that he had been tricked by the wise men, he was infuriated, and he sent and killed all the children in and around Bethlehem who were two years old or under....

On Christmas Eve a year ago, in very mysterious circumstances, a little cat named Willie came to live with us. Willie had been badly abused, starved within an inch of his life, and abandoned. But in spite of the way he had been treated, he had a gentle and loving spirit. He never asked for much, just a little piece of life and a place to live it. He had a good year with us. He filled out and he enjoyed life. But he was never strong, and despite everything we and the veterinarian could do, he slipped away from us the week before Christmas.

I tell you this because our experience with Willie hypersensitized me this past Christmas season as never before to the little ones, especially to the children, to the ones who suffer and die in silence. I have seen a lot and felt my skin grow tough with the years, but this Christmas I did not skim over the reports from Ethiopia—I read every word. I read about the climactic conditions and the political stupidity and the bureaucratic incompetence. I did not flip the channel, but watched the drawn faces and bloated bellies file past me.

I thought of all those whose gifts will never be shared with the world because they never had a chance; who, for lack of a cup of milk or a piece of bread, never had the chance to deliver whatever they might have received. When adults are oppressed and mistreated, they have a way of fighting back. I remember the 1971 movie *Tell Them Willie Boy Is Here*, in which a young Native American, oppressed and abused, finally goes on a rampage that, if nothing else, tells us he was here. But how do the little ones tell us they were here? How do they make us hear? We can shout our outrage when we are mistreated; we can tell them we are here. But what of the ones with no complaint? What of the desperate prayer of Margaret Brown: "Dear Father, guard with tenderness small things that have no words"?[39]

---

[39]Margaret Wise Brown, *A Child's Good Night Book* (Reading, MA: Young Scott Books, 1950), 27.

"When Herod saw that he had been tricked by the wise men, he was infuriated, and he sent and killed all the children in and around Bethlehem who were two years old or under...." Considering what we know about Herod, the slaughter of the innocents, although it has no extra-biblical witness, is considered by scholars to have been quite possible. If this slaughter took place, and I have no reason to doubt it, then it follows that Jesus had to have known. In an oral culture such as his, he could not have grown to manhood without hearing the story of the slaughter of the babies of Bethlehem. He had to know that they had died in his place. Could it be, then, that part of what he did was for them, was done in memory of them?

It seems that our responsibility is twofold when we think on these things. The first is to save those we can. The second responsibility is more delicate. If you read history or even a newspaper, you know that we cannot save them all. In spite of everything we do, we will lose many—too many. Which poses the question: What do we owe to those we cannot save? At least two things.

One. They must know before they die that somebody loved them. This was the work of Father Damien among the victims of Hansen's disease on Molokai. It was the work of Mickey Leland among the starving of Ethiopia. It remains the work of Mother Teresa of Calcutta, and it is a work to be affirmed. *Two*. In the blessed memory of those we lost, we must work for those who remain.

As we come to the table today, in memory of the One who died for us, may we take a moment to remember those who died for him, and then commit ourselves to that which we can do, in memory of them, to save those who have no words. As for this day, remember. The babies in the region of Bethlehem were here. Willie was here. The children of Auschwitz, Buchenwald, Treblinka, and Dachau were here. The little ones of Ethiopia were here. Jesus was here.

And I told you.

26 BREAD AND STONES
Matthew 4:1–5; 7:7–11

The tempter came and said to him, "If you are the Son of God, command these stones to become loaves of bread...." [Jesus said,] "Is there anyone among you who, if your child asks for bread, will give a stone?"

Palestine is a rocky land. And the rocks of the Holy Land figure prominently in the imagery of the Bible. In the first mention of bread in the New Testament, a very hungry Jesus was tempted to turn stones into bread. Shortly thereafter, in the Sermon on the Mount, Jesus asked the people if, when their children were hungry for bread, they would give them stones. The placement of these texts, relatively close together, is thought-provoking.

Bread was of infinitely more value than stones to the people of first-century Palestine. It still is, especially for those who are hungry. And yet, in both texts, Jesus shows that the value-distance between bread and stones is small compared to the distance between bread and the word of God. "One does not live by bread alone, but by every word that comes from the mouth of God" (4:4). "If you then, who are evil, know how to give good gifts to your children, how much more will your Father in heaven give good things to those who ask him" (7:11).

We share this bread this morning, and I vastly prefer it to rocks. Nevertheless, being bread, it can remind us of the responsibility that those who have bread bear. How can it do that? By what happens when we break it, not as an end in itself, but in quest for that word of God which calls us to love and service.

27 EATING WITH SINNERS
Matthew 9:10–13

And as he sat at dinner in the house, many tax collectors and sinners came and were sitting with him and his disciples. When the Pharisees saw this, they said to his disciples, "Why does your teacher eat with tax collectors and sinners?"

Parents are right. If you run with the wrong crowd, you get into trouble. Jesus certainly did. But what is different about his action is that Jesus did not seek what sinners could do for him, but rather what he could do for them. And because he did not exclude sinners, even Judas, from his table, we know that we have a place there also.

My tendency, perhaps yours, too, is to seek out those I like, those who see things the same way I do. Some evangelism programs acknowledge this up front, by saying that we "win" those who are most like us. I do not dispute that, but the gospel certainly does. Jesus was a good observant Jew, but he sought out tax collectors and sinners, ate with them, and shared the good news of God with them. He has also had followers, like William and Catherine Booth of the Salvation Army, who did the same.

One of the benefits of this table, apart from our personal communion-time with God, is that we eat here with sinners. And those who eat with us do the same. From time to time we need to be reminded of that. We do not gather to eat out of our perfection, but out of our weakness. Eating with sinners, as we do, can get us into trouble: the trouble of reaching out and bearing one another's burdens.

This table does not blot out or blur the conflicts between us. It sets them right out in the light where we can see them, and we see them in the illuminating light of the much-suffering man who extends bread and wine to us even as we betray him by our disdain of the sinner next to us. Yes, eating at this table with sinners can get us into trouble, the trouble that comes when greater self-awareness encounters a growing awareness of other selves, their needs, and our responsibilities to them. Another name for this trouble is...salvation.

28   MISSING THE POINT
Matthew 16:5–16

When the disciples reached the other side, they had forgotten to bring any bread. Jesus said to them, "Watch out, and beware of the yeast of the Pharisees and Sadducees." They said to one another, "It is because we have brought no bread." And becoming aware of it, Jesus said, "You of little faith.... How could you fail to perceive that I was not speaking about bread?"

I had just returned to Texas after almost two decades away. I was listening to a sermon in worship one day. The preacher returned again and again to a refrain that he delivered with inflection: "Impair us, O Lord, to do your will!" Although I was having trouble fitting the refrain to the rest of the sermon, it was nevertheless an intriguing point. Impair us. A wounded-like-Christ, thorn-in-the-side-like-Paul kind of thing. Slain-in-the-Spirit to do God's will. Not my normal approach, but interesting. Shaking hands after worship, I complimented the preacher on this thought-provoking assertion. He stared at me as if I was crazy and finally broke in: "What I said was, '*Empower* us, O Lord, to do your will.'"

Oh. Too long gone from Texas. I had gotten something from the message, perhaps even something helpful. But I had missed *his* point.

What we perceive is colored by our situation, our understanding, even our accent. The disciples had forgotten to bring bread for their journey, and they were hungry. So, as Jesus began telling them to beware the yeast of the Pharisees and Sadducees, they assumed he was rebuking them for having forgotten the bread. But Jesus was not talking about bread at all. He was warning them about the teachings of the Pharisees and Sadducees. And they missed his point altogether.

How do we perceive this table? The poor and hungry will perceive communion in one way, the rich and satiated in another; the contented in one way, the anxiety-ridden in another. As we meditate on the many symbols and meanings available at this table, let us do our best not to miss *his* point: "This is my body broken for you. Do this in remembrance of me."

29   IS IT I, LORD?
Matthew 26:20–21

When it was evening, he sat at table with the twelve disciples, and as they were eating, he said, "Truly I say to you, one of you will betray me." And they were very sorrowful, and began to say to him one after another, "Is it I, Lord?" (RSV)

Recently we went to see an amateur production of *Godspell*, the musical based upon the Gospel According to Matthew. The young people did a wonderful job. Having seen the musical before, I was able to sit back this time and just let the play happen to me. So it was in the course of the play that I caught a new glimpse of something I had seen a thousand times before, but never seriously considered. "'Truly I say to you, one of you will betray me.' And they were very sorrowful and began to say to him one after another, 'Is it I, Lord?'"

Is that not strange? Here is a group of twelve people who have left home, family, and occupation to follow this man around the country for three years; they have been totally committed to him and his message. Now he says that one of them is going to betray him, and I wonder why they didn't scream in unison: "No...NEVER!" But they did not. They said, "Is it I, Lord?" Which means something very interesting. It means that each of them realized within himself the potential for betrayal. There would be no reason for any one of them to ask if he were to be the betrayer unless he realized that he could be.

If I were to say, "Truly, one of you will go out after church and commit a serious crime," you might either laugh or tell me how stupid I was. But if I said that and then, one after the other, you came up to me and said, "Is it I?" that would be different. With this one question Peter and Andrew and James and John and Philip and Bartholomew and Thomas and Matthew and James and Thaddeus and Simon and Judas all confess that they could betray him.

And they sat and they were sad and frightened. And then Judas says, "Is it I, Master?" and Jesus says "You have said so," and we can almost hear eleven people say in unison, "Whew!" I suspect that the very first reaction of the disciples to Jesus' announcing Judas as the betrayer was not sorrow or anger or indignation, but rather relief. "Yes, it sure is sad about the Lord being betrayed. But it is not I. I would never, never do such a thing. I would die first. And I always was suspicious of old Judas. He never was any good, anyway." Cock-a-doodle-do.

The point is this—for the eleven disciples and for us: Judas did it. But we could have. And we therefore have no right to take comfort in his tragedy. We follow in the footsteps of the disciples, and one of our best developed skills is the avoidance of blame and responsibility. Nothing is ever our fault. Either we did not do it. Or we were framed. Or we were led down the path by someone else and thus not responsible for our actions. Shortly after we moved to California in the late 1970s, I attended a regional assembly of the Christian Church in the Pacific Southwest. The Jonestown tragedy had just occurred, and the agony was particularly acute for us since Jim Jones was an ordained minister of the Christian Church and had standing in our region. The assembly quickly passed a resolution lamenting the tragedy but denying any responsibility for it. I was more than a little ashamed.

I believe that one of the messages woven into the very fabric of the Lord's Supper is that this attitude of ours is wrong. Because when Jesus announced Judas as the betrayer the very next thing he did was to reach out to him with a loaf of bread. And if it had been you or I—and it could have been—I believe he would have done the same for us. I did not want Jesus to die, and I am not proud of how my concern at that moment was for myself, how relieved I was at not being named the betrayer. But it happened. And now I am called, with you, to claim my sin, to repent of it, and to come to the table. We may feel unworthy and want to shrink from confronting him here, but down through the years he continues to call to us on the last night of his life, to invite us to the table, to stretch out his hand to offer us bread, the blessed bread of forgiveness.

30 NEW WINESKINS
Mark 2:18–22

No one puts new wine into old wineskins; otherwise, the wine will burst the skins, and the wine is lost, and so are the skins; but one puts new wine into fresh wineskins.

I was among a pool of jurors being questioned by attorneys during *voir dire*. The attorneys were perusing the questionnaires we had completed about ourselves and our interests. In a stab at levity, the prosecutor said to one potential juror, "I see you subscribe to a magazine called *New Wine*. Are you a connoisseur?" The man replied, "It's a...Christian magazine." The courtroom response was fascinating. Half the crowd roared with laughter; half stared blankly, not comprehending; and the red-faced prosecutor was not a little embarrassed.

I suspect the response to Jesus' original remark was similar. "No, my disciples don't fast. You don't put new wine into old wineskins. New truth requires new forms." The outrageous, perhaps even blasphemous, nature of Jesus' claim would have surely startled, bemused, or confused his hearers. What new truth? What new forms?

The Eucharist is now a very old wineskin. It is celebrated in thousands of places in thousands of ways. Will the day come when it will need to be replaced? Yes. When Jesus returns and we see him face to face, there will be no need for a ritual to remember him by. We will delight in his living presence at the great banquet of God. In the meantime this old wineskin still works. It is well-stretched and has a few leaks, but it still works. And the old wine of Christ's love and sacrifice is new every morning on the lips of those who believe.

31 BREAD IN THE WILDERNESS
Mark 6:30–41

Taking the five loaves and the two fish, he looked up to heaven, and blessed and broke the loaves, and gave them to his disciples to set before the people; and he divided the two fish among them all.

The feeding of the five thousand is the only miracle of Jesus reported in all Four Gospels. It early became an important part of the Jesus story. Many themes are present. Lamar Williamson tells us that the feeding "... points back to Moses and the manna in the wilderness and forward to the messianic feast at the end-time, while the words describing

Jesus' prayer and the breaking of bread tie the scene contemporane-
ously to the Lord's Supper."[40]

Most of the great religions of the world have come "out of the wilderness." Christianity is no exception. Perhaps that is because truth is
more thinly veiled there, without the distractions of the city. There is,
however, danger in the wilderness: hunger, thirst, death. Here we find
that when we follow Jesus into the wilderness, the dangers are there, but
we are not alone. Others have come also. And there is Jesus, offering us
good news and, more than that, bread for the journey home.

This table is spread in the middle of town. But we still come apart to
"a lonely place" when we gather about it. It is good to find friends here.
It is good to meet Jesus here. And it is good to have this bread in the
wilderness for our long journey home.

---

[40]Lamar Williamson, *Mark* (Atlanta: John Knox, 1983), 128.

32   SALAD DAYS
Mark 6:42–44

*And all ate and were filled; and they took up twelve baskets full of
broken pieces and of the fish. Those who had eaten the loaves
numbered five thousand....*

It has been a great ride, but the party is over. No more pizza and
chicken-fried steak, washed down with Coke and balanced with Alka-
Seltzer. It is rabbit food these days, along with the counting of calories,
fat, and sodium. I suspect I am not alone in this, living on mere fragments of what I used to eat. I take some comfort, and counsel, from
Calvin: "If it please God to cut off our morsel and feed us but poorly, we
must be content with it, and pray God to give us patience when we have
not what our appetites crave."[41]

Yes, God, give us patience. Sometimes I wonder why the days of
youthful exuberance and indiscretion are called "salad days." No, the
salad days come later, when too many cheeseburgers and french fries
have done their damage. Here, then, is the grace. There is food for thought
if not for palate in this little text. After the overflowing bounty extended
in the feeding of the five thousand, where they all ate and were satisfied, the fragments left over were not thrown away, but gathered into
twelve baskets.

---

[41]John Calvin, "The Word Our Only Rule," reprinted in *20 Centuries of Great
Preaching*, eds. Clyde E. Fant, Jr. and William M. Pinson, Jr. (Waco:Word, 1971),
II:147.

Intended by the gospel writers to indicate the size of the grace involved, there is a corollary unsaid but implied. There is still much nourishment remaining. Many will continue to eat and benefit from the leftovers. When Jesus walked this earth, full of God's grace and truth, it was a rich feast of spirit for those who followed him. But that was a long time ago. What remains are the fragmentary accounts of his life and ministry we have in scripture, together with the broken pieces of bread we have at this table to remember him by.

Someone once asked feminist scholar Phyllis Trible why she spent so much time with scripture when there are so few fulfilling stories about women there. She replied, "When found, richly blessed, and fed upon, these remnant traditions provide more than enough sustenance for life."[42] And these fragments before us today, the blessed residue of Jesus' earthly sojourn, can still feed our spirits till we want no more.

---

[42]Phyllis Trible, "Five Loaves and Two Fishes: Feminist Hermeneutics and Biblical Theology," *Theological Studies* 50 (1989), 295.

33 "THEY WILL FAST IN THOSE DAYS"
Luke 5:33–35

Then they said to him, "John's disciples, like the disciples of the Pharisees, frequently fast and pray, but your disciples eat and drink." Jesus said to them, "You cannot make wedding guests fast while the bridegroom is with them, can you? The days will come when the bridegroom will be taken away from them, and then they will fast in those days."

Many Christians prefer, and some denominations require them, to fast prior to receiving the Lord's Supper. This is a commendable practice, but perhaps not for the reasons we think. Fasting as a discipline is sometimes seen as a way to lose weight, although it is not very effective unless a person's long-term lifestyle changes. As a spiritual discipline, fasting is viewed as a cleansing process that leads to a heightened awareness of God's presence and a deeper spiritual clarity.

But these are all secondary concerns. At base, fasting is a rehearsal for death, a reminder of the time that comes when no one eats or drinks.[43] Jesus' statement to his questioners that the time would come when his followers would fast is a two-edged sword. We will refrain from food in recognition of the "Bridegroom's" absence, but we will also follow him in the experience of death.

With this understanding, fasting before partaking of the Supper is a way to intensify that experience for us. Jesus did not only give us the bread and the cup—he died for us. Will we die for him...and in him?

---

[43]I owe this understanding to Fr. Charles Calabrese.

34 THE FATTED CALF
Luke 15:11–32

And get the fatted calf and kill it, and let us eat and celebrate; for this son of mine was dead and is alive again; he was lost and is found!

If the entire Bible were to be taken from us, I submit that our faith tradition could endure if we were but spared the parable of the prodigal. It is truly a parable for the ages, one rich in content and imagery, and translatable into a multitude of contexts. As I said to a group recently, I have heard sermons on the prodigal preached from the perspective of the son, of the father, of the elder brother. I have even heard a sermon preached from the perspective of the unmentioned mother. But I am still waiting to hear a sermon from the perspective of the fatted calf.

If you look at the parable from the fatted calf's perspective, it takes on a whole new meaning. And it is a meaning with large eucharistic overtones. In order for there to be a celebration, something has to die. To have abundant life, you must take life. We do it every day. We want to live, so fish, chickens, carrots, rutabagas must die. We gather round this table re-enacting this universal truth. The fatted calf, we suspect, did not know he was about to die that new life might be affirmed. But Jesus did. He gave his life that we might have ours. In our eating and drinking this day, we remember that and give thanks.

35 GO HOME. TRUST GOD.
Luke 23:44–46

It was now about noon, and darkness came over the whole land until three in the afternoon, while the sun's light failed; and the curtain of the temple was torn in two. Then Jesus, crying with a loud voice, said, "Father, into your hands I commend my spirit." Having said this, he breathed his last.

This is the day that takes its measure of us. Goodness and truth, the very love of God, is nailed to a Roman cross. The one in whom we had placed all our hopes has breathed his last, and the sky turns black in the middle of a Friday afternoon. Good Friday is instructive on at least two levels. The first is universal as the great cosmic drama is played out upon a worldly stage. Mostly, though, this is theater that is beyond us, and we just watch and say like the centurion, "My God!" The other level though is very, very personal and can be framed in this question: What are we going to do? Whatever are we going to do now?

There are two traditional answers to this question in scripture and in the church. The first is "run and hide." That is what the disciples did. And it is hard to blame them. That is what most of us do when the going gets rough. Our faith is a fair-weather affair: we are happy to give God the glory as long as God gives us whatever it is that we want. But when the cookie jar runs out, so do we. Scot preacher Arthur John Gossip could never understand this kind of faith. Preaching after the sudden death of his wife, he wondered about those who, at the first sign of trouble, "fling peevishly" from the Christian faith. "In God's name," said Gossip, "fling to what?"[44]

I was sitting in the dentist's chair not long ago, listening to the dentist tell me about her dream of the night before. (I was a rather captive audience.) She was running away from an alligator that was chasing her. Every few steps she would turn around and hit the alligator on the snout with a club. It would stop, she would run on, turn around, and there it was, still coming after her. In one way or another, most of us have this dream from time to time. Running away. Somebody after us. Our feet and legs churning but not getting us anywhere. Deep within us is the need to run away and hide. But there is wisdom in our dreams because, in the long run, it never works. We can run away from Good Friday, but every time we turn around, there is the cross, and it is gaining on us.

The other answer to the question of what we are going to do on Good Friday is more popular these days, among preachers and laypeople alike, and it is often expressed in the popular phrase, "It's Friday, but Sunday's coming." The way you deal with Friday is to make a proleptic leap from Palm Sunday over Friday to Easter Day, keeping your faith and your spirits intact. The classical exposition of this is found in Charles Goff's famous sermon, "Anyone for Calvary."[45] Goff tells about being a seminary student in Chicago back during the Depression. He used to ride the elevated train to his little church out in the country. One of the stops on the train just outside the city was Calvary Cemetery. The conductor would walk through the train saying, "Calvary next. Anyone for Calvary?" As Goff tells it, there was hardly ever anyone for Calvary. Oh, sometimes during the day there would be someone with flowers who got off, but never at night, for it was dark and forbidding and dangerous there. One night, however, Goff was riding the train when something different happened. "Anyone for Calvary?" the conductor asked as usual. This time a man got up and got off when the train stopped. Goff was so surprised he looked out the window to see that a new apartment house had risen on the other side of the cemetery. There was a light on in one of the apartments; a woman and child stood there silhouetted by the light. They waved to the man. He waved back and began walking. So is death swallowed up in life. "It's Friday, but Sunday's coming."

---

[44]Arthur John Gossip, "But When Life Tumbles In, What Then?" in Fant and Pinson, VIII:235.

[45]See Charles Ray Goff, *Anyone for Calvary* (Westwood, NJ: Revell, 1958), 14-18.

And that is good, except for one thing. The disciples of Jesus did not know that Sunday was coming. All they knew was that it was Friday, and the too easy jump that many of us make to Sunday can rob Friday and the cross of its power and meaning. One of the real benefits of the noonday services held all these many years is the way it forces us to encounter Holy Week in all its emotions, not just a couple. Most Christians jump from the joy of Palm Sunday's triumphal entry to the joy of Easter's resurrection with nary a stop in between, not realizing that the primary essential requirement for resurrection is death. "Anyone for Calvary?" is an important question.

So I want to make one last suggestion, one that comes from reflecting on a story attached to our text. There is a tradition I heard about years ago that says when darkness came over the whole land as Jesus was crucified, "the good women of Jerusalem lit their Sabbath lamps."[46] They lit their Sabbath lamps. This tradition is generally remembered as a putdown, of either Jews or women or both, saying that they were so indifferent to Jesus that when the sky turned black in the middle of a Friday afternoon, when heaven and earth clashed like thunder, rocks were split, the temple curtain was torn, trees were uprooted, everything was being turned upside down, when the signs of Armageddon were everywhere around, the good women of Jerusalem missed it and blithely went about their business, first pausing to light their Sabbath lamps. Silly Jewish women!

It was not until much later that I decided that the response of these women may be the key to our own response to Good Friday. Because what would you have had them do? When everything goes wrong, when your world has been turned upside down, when there is an other-worldly electricity in the air and the sky turns dark, what would you have had them do? Run and hide, like the disciples? Laugh it off with a look ahead to better days a'coming? Or do that one thing that you can do that affirms, "I do not know what is going on, but I trust God. My world may end, the mountains may collapse in the midst of the sea, and the stars begin to fall, but I light this lamp remembering how it was God who led us out of the land of Egypt, who parted the Red Sea, who fed us manna in the desert, who sustained us for forty years in the wilderness, who protected us against our enemies when we came into the land. Therefore, whatever cataclysm may now be upon us, I light this lamp trusting that the same God who was with then will be with us now." James Sanders once said that the key to understanding the stories of scripture lies in our looking not only at the actions of Jesus but also at the actions of those those who were about him. And the one act of faith in the whole larger Passion story is that of the good women of Jerusalem.

---

[46]I first heard this story from Ronald Osborn.

The much lamented Ed Wright once said that the only hope for us after Friday is that we are facing in the right direction if and when God should choose to act again.[47] And so the message for Good Friday is perhaps the simplest of all the days of this week. No call to action today. No ethical imperatives. No maudlin despair. No blithe sunny look ahead. Just come to the table. Remember who you are and what God has done for you. Then go home. Light the lamps of your own faith against the gathering darkness. And trust God. This is bottom-line day. *De profundis.* Bedrock. If God cannot be trusted, then nothing else matters. If God can be trusted, then nothing else matters. Go home and trust God. I do not know how. I do not even know why. But everything is going to be all right.

---

[47]Remembered from a sermon preached by Ed Wright many years ago.

36 RECOGNITION AND RENEWAL
Luke 24:13–35

... they urged him strongly, saying, "Stay with us, because it is almost evening and the day is now nearly over...." When he was at the table with them, he took bread, blessed and broke it, and gave it to them. Then their eyes were opened, and they recognized him;...That same hour they got up and returned to Jerusalem....

The focus of this marvelous story about Jesus' post-resurrection walk to Emmaus[48] with two disciples is generally upon the last verse of the story. The disciples walked a good while with Jesus but did not recognize him. It was not until he sat at the table and broke bread that their eyes were opened and they realized it was Jesus. So the disciples returned to Jerusalem and told the others "what had happened on the road, and how he had been made known to them in the breaking of the bread" (v. 35).

As the bread is broken, something happens—that something is recognition. Good point. The breaking of bread in the community of faith remains an eye-opening experience for so many of us. We are often graced by an awareness we did not have a few minutes before. And that is something for which we are thankful. But recognition is not the only thing that happens when the bread is broken in this story.

Consider. When they arrived at Emmaus, Jesus appeared to be going on. But the disciples encouraged him to stop, eat, and spend the

---

[48]Scholars are unable to locate Emmaus. For a marvelous sermon on this text which grows from that problem, see "Emmaus" in *New Life for the Old, Old Story* by Amanda Burr (Arlington, VA: Thornsbury, Bailey & Brown, 1989), 163-176.

night with them. Why? Because "it is almost evening and the day is now nearly over" (v. 29). Before they experienced the presence of the resurrected Christ, it was late and getting dark. The disciples said that they "had hoped that he was the one," but now he was dead, for them, both literally and figuratively, the day was over and the darkness had come. But look what happens after the recognition at the table. "That same hour they got up and returned to Jerusalem" (v. 33). After they experience the resurrected Christ, it is no longer late, no longer dark.[49] Their spirits have also been resurrected, and they return to action. So the blessing of this story lies not only in its implication that the Eucharist is eye-opening, but also in its witness to the energizing effect of that recognition. Sometimes we too may feel that our "day" is nearly over, but here at this table we find the renewal we need to get back on the road again that we might tell everyone the news: "We have seen the Lord!"

---

[49]I am indebted for this insight into the text to Mr. Eddie Smart, pastor of the Wesley Memorial United Methodist Church in Cleburne, Texas.

37   IT ALL BEGAN AT CANA
John 2:1–11

"Everyone serves the good wine first, and then the inferior wine after the guests have become drunk. But you have kept the good wine until now." Jesus did this, the first of his signs, in Cana of Galilee; and revealed his glory; and his disciples believed in him.

The story of Jesus changing water into wine at the wedding feast in Cana is one filled, in Raymond Brown's words, with "an embarrassment of riches."[50] There are many things to ponder in this text. Here is one of them. John's gospel carefully ties together three separate events in Jesus' life: the wedding at Cana ["My hour has not yet come" (2:4)]; the feeding of the five thousand ["Now the Passover, the festival of the Jews, was near" (6:4)]; and the Passover meal itself ["Now before the festival of the Passover, Jesus knew that his hour had come to depart from this world" (13:1)]. The wine of the wedding, the bread of the mass feeding, the wine and bread of the last supper: these images are spread across the gospel, pointing to the critical hour to come.[51]

The case can be made that John's whole gospel is then a kind of eucharistic meditation, a getting-ready for what is to come. So through bread and wine, we can best remember who Jesus was and all these

---

[50]Raymond E. Brown, *The Gospel according to John, I-XII* (Garden City, NY: Doubleday, 1966), 103.

[51]*Ibid.,* 110.

things that Jesus did. And it all began at Cana. Why would John tell this strange and difficult story to mark the beginning of Jesus' ministry? Possibly because it fits his overall purpose, and also because the metaphor is irresistible. The chief steward's remark to the unsuspecting bridegroom, "You have kept the good wine until now," may be on John's part both an affirmation that the Messianic Age is now arriving and that many will wrongly ascribe its glory. The steward thinks the bridegroom is responsible for this good fortune. But it is Jesus.

Many people today look in all kinds of directions for good news and salvation: systems, seers, themselves. But it is still Jesus. Here at the table we remember that. It all begins here.

38 WATER, WATER, WORLD, AND WINE
Genesis 1:1–2

In the beginning when God created the heavens and the earth, the earth was a formless void and darkness covered the face of the deep, while a wind from God swept over the face of the waters.

John 2:6–7

Now standing there were six stone water jars, for the Jewish rites of purification, each holding twenty or thirty gallons. Jesus said to them, "Fill the jars with water." And they filled them up to the brim.

Here is another fascinating parallel—between the miracle at Cana and the miracle at creation. The Bible story begins in Genesis with water, lots of water. And God's first act was to move over the chaotic waters, shaping and bordering them, that earth might become hospitable to life. The action in the Gospel According to John begins in water, as Jesus submits to baptism, and immediately moves to the wedding feast at Cana. In response to a crisis, Jesus takes water, as God earlier did, and re-shapes it into what is now needed: wine for the feast.[52]

Thus the most ordinary of worldly things—water, present since creation—becomes the symbol of God's and Jesus' creating, transforming power. And we see further how that most ordinary of things—a human being—was reshaped by God into a Savior for all. God chose water with which to begin creation; Jesus chose water with which to begin his ministry. God chose Jesus to redeem creation. And this memorial feast reminds us that Jesus chose us to continue that work of redemption. Chose us and gave himself for us. There used to be water in this chalice,

---

[52]See Sister Vandana, "Water—God's Extravaganza: John 2.1–11," in *Voices from the Margin: Interpreting the Bible in the Third World*, ed. R. S. Sugirtharajah (Maryknoll, NY: Orbis, 1991), 118-119.

but it has been reshaped by Jesus into the wine of memory and salvation. God, reshape us now to do your will; Jesus, change us now as you need to do your work.

This final thought: could it be that the miracle did not occur until what-had-been-water was actually poured out? Could it be that the miracle for us, the transformation of our lives that we long for, will not occur until our lives are poured out in service and love?

39   THE WELLS OF SAMARIA
John 4:1–6

Jesus left Judea and started back to Galilee. But he had to go through Samaria.

John 4:3 says of Jesus, "He left Judea and started to Galilee." That is a powerful verse. The heritage and destiny of Jesus. Born in Judea, physically and spiritually, for it says in scripture that from you, Bethlehem in the land of Judea, shall come the one who will rule over Israel (Matthew 2:6). And Galilee. What did the angel say to the women at the tomb? "He is not here; for he has been raised...and is going before you to Galilee" (Matthew 28:6-7). Beautiful.

Verse 4, however, tears it. "But he had to go through Samaria." Samaria was a district in which Jesus had no special interest; it just lay between where he was and where he was going. Henry Sloane Coffin suggested that Samaria is a metaphor for routine, that through which we all have to go to get where we want to be.[53] Samaria is the dishes and the laundry and the grocery store, the school, the shop, and the church— those things through which we must go.

Look, though, at what happened to Jesus there. He found four wells to drink from. First was Jacob's well, the source of refreshment for weary travelers. Second was his encounter with the woman at the well, where the meaning of living water was explained. Third were the people who came out to hear him teach and reinforced his understanding of his own identity. And fourth, perhaps even unknown to Jesus at the time, was that well which watered the seed that would grow to become the parable of the good Samaritan. When we plod faithfully through the Samaria of our routine, similar wells disclose themselves and convince us that the Spirit of God is at work.

Well, here we are again at the table. I wonder what will happen today. Drink deep of the wells of Christ.

---

[53]Henry Sloane Coffin, *Communion through Preaching* (New York: Charles Scribner's Sons, 1952), 43-44.

40 THIRST
John 4:7–15

Everyone who drinks of this water will be thirsty again, but those who drink of the water that I give them will never be thirsty.

Wretched thirst. We think of the man crawling in the desert who would give everything for a drink of water. We have seen pictures of those who have died of thirst, contorted and in agony. So when Jesus offers us water that will allow us to thirst no more, we know that is a marvelous thing. It makes me wonder, though. If it is living water that symbolizes the message of Jesus, then why at the Last Supper did he offer his followers wine to remember him by? To borrow a phrase, people cannot live on wine alone. Wine is not a thirst-quencher. The more wine consumed, the thirstier people can become. But maybe that is the point. The living water of Christ is eternal, once for all. But we must continue to live day to day. And we know that, on a daily basis, thirst is a good thing. It is our bodies' way of telling us they need fluids. Without thirst we would risk dehydration. Without a spiritual thirst we might not continue to climb higher in our quest for God. Chrysostom put it this way fifteen hundred years ago:

> It is the same with you as with the friends of wine at a worldly feast: the more they drink, the thirstier they become. And the more I pour out for you the wine of learning, the stronger is your desire for it, and the thirstier you become. Therefore I do not cease to imitate the host, and offer a richly set table, and pitchers filled with the wine of learning. For I see that when you have drunk it all up, nevertheless you still go home thirsty.[54]

What Chrysostom affirms for preaching, I affirm for communion. How many thousands of times have we come to the table to remember him? I can hardly wait to come here again. I thirst. For his mercy and his love. For the companionship we share as we come together, needy beggars that we are. Everyone knows that Jesus turned water into wine. Perhaps the greater miracle, and one not yet universally acknowledged, is that Jesus can turn wine into water, the wonderful living water which assuages thirst forever.

---

[54]John of Antioch, Chrysostom, in Chrysostomus Baur, *John Chrysostom and His Time* (Westminster, MD: Newman Press, 1959), I:216.

41 HEAVENLY FOOD
John 6:30–35

"Very truly, I tell you, it was not Moses who gave you the bread from heaven, but it is my Father who gives you the true bread from heaven...." They said to him, "Sir, give us this bread always." Jesus said to them, "I am the bread of life...."

The specter of hunger hovers over our world like an evil angel. For some there is too much food; for many others there is not enough. Mohandas Gandhi spoke for those "many others" when he said, "To the millions who have to go without two meals a day the only acceptable form in which God dare appear is food."[55] It is so tempting at this table to reply, "Yes, but it has already happened!" Do you remember the carol we sing at Christmastime?

> King of Kings, yet born of Mary,
> As of old on earth he stood,
> Lord of Lords in human vesture,
> In the body and the blood,
> He will give to all the faithful
> His own self for heavenly food.[56]

What does it mean for John and for us to say that Christ is our heavenly food, that Christ is the Bread of Life? It means nothing if we tell a mother and her starving children that Christ will be their food, and then walk away in a self-satisfied way. But it means everything if we ourselves are transformed by that understanding, that the Christ we take into ourselves changes us to more adequately reflect the nature of Christ. Monica Hellwig writes:

> When Jesus compares himself with the manna in the desert and calls himself bread for the life of the world, it certainly implies that what he gives is to be received by sharing.... In the person of Jesus there is a breakthrough into a way of life that is constituted by trust and sharing .... In the person of Jesus there is a breakthrough into a way of life that is constituted by trust and sharing and concern for others....[57]

She goes on to say that "to accept the bread of the Eucharist is to accept to be bread and sustenance for the poor of the world."[58] You are what you eat. To eat this bread is to be that bread for others, to serve in Christ's place for those who need him. Sometimes that means bringing a word

---

[55]Mohandas Gandhi, in Gerald Kennedy, *My Third Reader's Notebook* (Nashville: Abingdon, 1974), 85-86.

[56]"Let All Mortal Flesh Keep Silence," traditional French carol based upon the Liturgy of St. James.

[57]Monica K. Hellwig, *The Eucharist and the Hunger of the World* (New York: Paulist, 1976), 30-32.

[58]*Ibid.*, 78.

of encouragement; sometimes it means bringing a loaf of bread. Always it means seeing the gifts of Christ holistically, for the real needs of the world: spiritual and physical. To do less is to deny the very incarnation that forms the basis for our faith.

42 COMMUNION AND CANNIBALISM
John 6:52–58

"Very truly, I tell you, unless you eat the flesh of the Son of Man and drink his blood, you have no life in you."

There is one aspect of the Eucharist about which many have thought, but almost none have spoken. I wish Jesus had not said the things he is reported to have said in John 6:52-58. But there it is: eat the flesh of the Son of Man; drink his blood. One word for that is cannibalism. Early Christians were often attacked as "flesh-eaters." And there are few things that arouse more horror in us. Jerome Ellison in *Report to the Creator* and Rudolph Raber in *Tenderly to Jerusalem* have spoken about it and given me courage to do the same. Ellison poses the problem in historical context. A favorite objection of skeptics, he says is that:

> ... in the most primitive times, men superstitiously believed that when they ate the flesh and drank the blood of a strong or wise man they gained in the deceased's qualities of strength and wisdom. To carry on such a cannibalistic practice, say these critics, is to outrage reason.[59]

Raber places the issue in more personal context:

> The whole idea [of cannibalism] is a repugnant one and ugly to the point of nausea. To think of eating the flesh and drinking the blood of another human being is almost more than our civilized minds and stomachs can bear.[60]

Ellison and Raber go on to suggest that, while we are not literally ingesting human flesh and blood, there is indeed a cannibalistic undertone to the Eucharist. Why? Because, in spite of our protestations to the contrary, we are cannibals! We are the devourers of all good things. We devour the planet. We devour each other. We would devour God if we could. And, in truth, we did at Calvary: "human sin took the Son of God and devoured him in death."[61]

But God's love, which always meets us in our sin and offers mercy, did not abandon us, even in our sadistic murder of Jesus: "Here, You say, this is My body, work out your sadism on this, while I continue to

---

[59]Jerome Ellison, *Report to the Creator* (New York: Harper, 1955), 208.
[60]Rudolph W. Raber, *Tenderly to Jerusalem* (St. Louis: Eden, 1968), 68.
[61]Raber, 69.

love you."[62] What amazing grace. What wondrous love.

When we partake of the emblems of this sacrifice, we are reminded that when we did the very worst thing that we could have done to Jesus Christ and to God, the *very* worst, God and Jesus responded in love. While I do not understand love that strong, I am very grateful for it, and moved to be more loving in return.

[62]Ellison, 209.

43 COME AND HAVE BREAKFAST
John 21:9–15

When they had gone ashore, they saw a charcoal fire there, with fish on it, and bread....Jesus said to them, "Come and have breakfast."

There are only two places in the New Testament where a charcoal fire is mentioned. The first is John 18:18, where Peter stands warming himself at the gate of the high priest after having denied knowing Jesus. The second is here, where Jesus invites Peter and the others to come and have breakfast.[63] Jesus, as was typical of him, appears offering food. Here it is the common meal called breakfast. The repetition of the use of a charcoal fire to cook it reminds us that the food is for a betrayer that Jesus still loves. Quite amazing, that. And true for us as well. How we have denied Jesus in our comings and goings, and yet here he is, with food and outstretched hands. Peter, surprised by grace, finally got the point. The surprises of God are not over. Just when we least expect it comes the smell of fish, cooking over a charcoal fire. May we also, receiving these gifts from one who still loves us, get the point and become the followers he calls us to be.

---

[63]I have dealt with this text in some detail in the *Biblical Preaching Journal* (Spring 1989), 6-9.

44 WHO MAY COME TO THE TABLE?
Acts 27:33–38

Just before daybreak, Paul urged all of them to take some food,...After he had said this, he took bread; and giving thanks to God in the presence of all, he broke it and began to eat. Then all of them were encouraged and took food for themselves.

Many have wondered about the eucharistic nature of this text. Was Paul really sharing the Lord's Supper with unbaptized sailors? Geoffrey

Wainwright suggests three possibilities for interpreting this text.[64] It may be that Paul was simply observing the Jewish custom of grace before meals. Or that Luke the author uses this incident as a prefigure of the Eucharist. The third, and most powerful, interpretation comes from Dutch missiologist J. C. Hoekendijk, who proposes that we understand this text as one which argues that no conditions should be set concerning who may partake of communion. "For every celebration of the Lord's supper is a sign erected of the great coming banquet, and God wishes His house to be full. The offer of communion is as open and free as the offer of the gospel: Whosoever will may come!"[65]

Wainwright, while moved by Hoekendijk's interpretation, is still concerned about the unbaptized at the table. So he suggests a compromise. No one should be refused admittance to the table. But he or she should be brought to baptism as soon as possible.[66] At first glance, this seems a little cold-blooded. But it need not be. It removes bars from the table, allowing whosoever will to come into the presence of God. And it further obliges the church to invite the communicant to confront the gospel and be baptized into Christ. That, after all, is what we are about.

Come to the table. Like the sailors on Paul's ship, you are welcome. But be warned. You may meet Christ here and be called into his service.

---

[64]Geoffrey Wainwright, *Eucharist and Eschatology* (New York: Oxford, 1981), 130-135.

[65]J. C. Hoekendijk, paraphrased by Wainwright, 131.

[66]Wainwright, 134.

45 THE CUP OF POISON
Romans 14:13–23

Do not let what you eat cause the ruin of one for whom Christ died....It is good not to eat meat or drink wine or do anything that makes your brother or sister stumble.

Communion was being served by intinction and I was holding the cup. One by one people filed by, dipped their bread in the cup, and partook. One man walked up, stood for a moment, and then leaned over and whispered in my ear: "Is it wine?" The situation was instantaneously clear, and I was able to smile and say "no." He smiled, received the Eucharist, and returned to his seat.

For most people at the Lord's Table, a chalice of wine is a cup of blessing. But, for a recovering alcoholic, it is a cup of poison. At least three things are at work here. First is Paul's admonition to the Romans here and to others elsewhere that, while all things may be "legal" for Christians, not all things are right, because of the effect they may have on others. We all have weaknesses; our life together in faith should not be one which feeds the weaknesses of some among us. Second, the fruit of the vine, that many receive without great thought, gives serious pause to an alcoholic. The wine represents blood that represents suffering. Wine also represents alcoholism that represents suffering. Recovering alcoholics feel this suffering at a deep and personal level.[67]

So while they may not drink the wine, they "feel" the wine and all it means. Third, would it not be helpful if all of us who come to the table would pause to consider our own weaknesses and how the love of God in Christ stretches forth to meet and help us there?

---

[67]This I have from a conversation with Max Jones, pastor of the First Christian Church in Granbury, Texas.

46 IN THE SAME NIGHT
1 Corinthians 11:23–26

For I received from the Lord what I also handed on to you, that the Lord Jesus on the night when he was betrayed took a loaf of bread, and when he had given thanks, he broke it and said, "This is my body that is for you. Do this in remembrance of me." In the same way he took the cup also, after supper, saying, "This cup is the new covenant in my blood. Do this, as often as you drink it, in remembrance of me." For as often as you eat this bread and drink the cup, you proclaim the Lord's death until he comes.

This is the great communion text, the warrant and authority for our service. The finest communion sermon I have ever heard was preached in James Chapel of Union Theological Seminary, New York, on Moratorium Day, 1969. The Vietnam War was raging. Almost weekly there was some form of protest at the seminary. During the height of this tension, Professor James Sanders preached a sermon and invited us to the table. His sermon, called "In the Same Night," was later published in his book *God Has a Story, Too.* I commend the sermon to you and offer these three affirmations from it, affirmations from a sermon that has helped shape my understanding of the Eucharist and my approach to this book.

1. It was on the night in which we betrayed him that he broke bread and gave it to us....[God's grace is expressed] in the midst of our sin: we know that God comes to us in our [act of] betrayal.

2. This was our night, the night the church was conceived. And we were all there, all twelve of us, seated about the table....I know of a certainty that because Judas was there I am not excluded. What if he

had not been present? Then that bread would not be for me.

3. No excuse…could possibly increase the love which there surrounds us or the forgiveness which there indicts us. And then we realize…that salvation is also judgment…the judgment of his grace: I do love you still.[68]

Thanks be to God for such persistent, gracious love.

---

[68]Reprinted from James A. Sanders, *God Has a Story, Too* (Philadelphia: Fortress, 1979), 94, 96, 100. Used with permission of Augsburg Fortress.

47 TOO BAD, STILL, TO COME TO THE TABLE?
1 Corinthians 11:27–29

Whoever, therefore, eats the bread or drinks the cup of the Lord in an unworthy manner will be answerable for the body and blood of the Lord. Examine yourselves, and only then eat of the bread and drink of the cup. For all who eat and drink without discerning the body eat and drink judgment against themselves.

If Paul had known the trouble these verses would cause the church, he might not have written them. Surely intended to keep people from turning the Lord's Supper into gluttonous, drunken events, where the significance of the ritual is lost in the revelry, this text has been turned into a Damoclean sword, warning people of the damnation that awaits them if they partake of the Eucharist "unworthily." As a result many honest and dedicated people, who feel unworthy of the body and blood of Christ, as all of us are, have refrained from going to the table.

During the radical, or leftwing, Reformation, a number of leaders suspended the Supper. Among them was spiritualist Caspar Schwenkfeld, who came to be identified with the practice of *stillstand*, "the suspension of the Supper until all groups could be brought to some accord as to its proper meaning and practice, while in the meantime defending it from defilement."[69] Schwenkfeld was concerned about his own unworthiness and more concerned about "casting that which is holy unto the dogs."[70]

Other stories through history reinforce the power of this text. Ralph Waldo Emerson left the church rather than serve communion. George Washington always stayed home from church on Communion Sunday.[71] Pastor John Claypool remembers that on the first Communion Sunday of his first pastorate in Kentucky, he was startled when but a few of the

---

[69]George Huntston Williams, *The Radical Reformation* (Philadelphia: Westminster, 1962), 114.

[70]Caspar Schwenkfeld, cited by Williams, ibid.

[71]Frank S. Mead, ed., *Communion Messages* (Westwood, NJ: Fleming H. Revell, 1961), 5.

congregation came forward to receive the Supper. He later learned that a previous severe pastor had frightened most of the people away from the table with warnings of damnation.[72]

I have two responses to this problem. First, I am glad that we have this text. While I do not believe every communion must be an intense spiritual experience or that we must be perfectly right with God before we partake, I do think that the impetus this text provides for critical personal reflection is a good thing. And there are no doubt times when refraining from partaking is proper for a person. *Not* doing something can sometimes be as important as doing it.

On the other hand, when this text is used as a hammer to keep people from the table, the very purpose of the Supper may be subverted. No one is worthy of Christ. All of us have sinned and fallen short. With this understanding I would have been more surprised, in the situation Claypool described, at the few who came to the table than I would at the large number who stayed away. I suggest that we *are* worthy not because of anything we may have done, but because of the very sacrifice that this table commemorates. Christ died not because we were without sin but that our sins might be forgiven. It is here that we testify to that and gather strength to journey toward worthiness.

During his second administration, Abraham Lincoln appointed a young man to a position in a government agency in Washington. In the interview with the president, the young man said, "Mr. President, I am not worthy of the honor." Lincoln looked up at him and said, "Then, sir, be worthy of it from now on."[73] Christ our passover is sacrificed for us. Come thoughtfully and thankfully to the table.

(See also Meditation #12.)

---

[72]John Claypool, from a sermon delivered on Good Friday, April 20, 1973, at First Christian Church, Fort Worth, Texas.

[73]A story attributed to Abraham Lincoln. I am unable to document the source.

48 FLESH, BLOOD AND PEACE
Ephesians 2:14–16; Colossians 1:15–20

For he is our peace; in his flesh he has made both groups into one and has broken down the dividing wall, that is, the hostility between us. He has abolished the law with its commandments and ordinances....For in him all the fullness of God was pleased to dwell, and through him God was pleased to reconcile to himself all things, whether on earth or in heaven, by making peace through the blood of his cross.

Yet more contradictions. How do you abolish hostility by giving up your body? How do you make peace by blood? It is a disorienting thought, like running for rest or eating for thinness. The jarring nature of the affirmation about the peace that Christ brings gets our attention. We do not make peace that way or even hope for peace that way. We think of peace in terms of harmony and good will, not flesh and blood.

But the Christian faith is a very materialistic and sensuous one. It affirms that the Word became flesh, that God was incarnate in Jesus Christ. We can:

- See him: "Behold the Lamb of God…!" (John 1:29, RSV)
- Hear him: "This is my beloved Son…listen to him." (Matthew 17:5 RSV)
- Taste him: "I am the living bread that came down from heaven. Whoever eats of this bread will live forever.…" (John 6:51)
- Touch him: "Touch me and see.…" (Luke 24:39)
- Even smell him in his followers: "For we are the aroma of Christ to God among those who are being saved.…" (2 Corinthians 2:15)

God has come to us in a way we did not expect and brought peace in a way we did not expect. From the beginning of the gospel story, where the shepherds in the field near Bethlehem heard angels sing of "peace on earth" (Luke 2:14), to the end "making peace by the blood of his cross" (Colossians 1:20), and beyond the end to the new beginning, when the risen Christ "came and stood among them and said 'Peace be with you'" (John 20:19), the peace of Christ, the *Pax Christi*, comes to us in a new and different way. It is not the peace of the world, but the peace of God. "…My peace I give to you. I do not give to you as the world gives" (John 14:27).

49 FOOD FOR TRAVELLERS
Hebrews 13:7–16

For here we have no lasting city, but we are looking for the city that is to come.

Msgr. Ronald Knox was a British chaplain and Bible translator who had a special gift for interpreting the Eucharist. In a book of his sermons called *The Window in the Wall: Reflections on the Holy Eucharist*, he says, with the writer to the Hebrews, that "we are born for eternity, that we have an everlasting city, but not here." He continues:

If we are on our journey, we must have provisions. And the language of the liturgy leaves us in no doubt what those provisions are. *Esca viatorum*, the food of travellers, *per tuas semitas duc nos quo tendimus*, bring us by thy own path, to our journey's end; *ecce panis angelorum factus cibus viatorum*, behold the bread of angels, sent to pilgrims in their banishment! *Qui vitam sine termino nobis donet in patria*, so we may pass eternity, poor exiles, on our native shore! The Holy Eucharist is our *viaticum*, our allowance of food at every stage in our travels; it is only by a gracious technicality that we reserve the name for that iron ration which will strengthen us for the last stage of all. Day by day and week by week, this is our appropriate nourishment.[74]

As one who loves to travel, both by car with supplies in the trunk and by foot with supplies on my back, I realize that food for travelling is different from food at the house. Travelling food must be both compact and nourishing. It must meet essential nutritional and social needs: good for stomach, palate, and sharing with comrades. There is neither time nor place for the decorative, insubstantial food of sedentary living.

The Eucharist is that kind of no-frills food: bread and cup, shared with neighbor in gratitude to God. It meets our need for spiritual nourishment on the journey and at the journey's end. A dear woman that I know had come to her last day. Her husband and nephew gently lifted her up in her bed, gave her a piece of bread, a sip of juice, and spoke to her of Jesus and heaven. She partook, lay gently back, and smiled. This journey was over. She had kept the faith. And she now had all the food she would need for the final journey. The journey home. Thanks be to God.

---

[74]Ronald A. Knox, *The Window in the Wall: Reflections on the Holy Eucharist* (New York: Sheed & Ward, 1956), 109-110.

50 BLOOD POLLUTES—AND SAVES—THE LAND 1 John 2:1–2

If anyone does sin, we have an advocate with the Father, Jesus Christ the righteous; and he is the atoning sacrifice for our sins, and not for ours only but also for the sins of the whole world.

Toward the end of the Book of Numbers, the legal code concerning murder is spelled out. It says that you shall not allow a murderer who has fled to his city of refuge to return. If you do so, you pollute the land in which you live, "for blood pollutes the land, and no expiation can be made for the land, for the blood that is shed in it, except by the blood of one who shed it" (35:33). In other words, the only thing that can cleanse the land of the pollution of murder is the blood of the murderer. The logic here is clear and understandable.

In the New Testament we encounter a strange twist on this old law, one that knifes through logic and threatens to disorient us. It is the blood of the murdered, the blood of Christ, that saves and cleanses, not the blood of those who killed him. And this understanding carried forward in the life and liturgy of the church. Tertullian wrote in the third century that "the blood of martyrs is the seed of the church,"[75] affirming the action of Jesus as model for Christian living and dying. And the 1989 *United Methodist Hymnbook* brings us to the table with these words from 1 John 2:1–2: "If anyone does sin, we have an advocate with the Father, Jesus Christ the righteous; and he is the atoning sacrifice for our sins, and not for ours only but also for the sins of the whole world."[76] The central message of Christ and of this table is therefore one of sacrificial love, not revenge.

Some continue to have problems with a faith based on such a reversal of logic, and I have been among them. The truth remains: if God were perfectly logical, there would be no chance for our being saved. I struggle to understand, but I come to places where I must bow my head in submission to One who is wiser than I. This is one of them: thanks be to God for the saving blood of Jesus Christ.

---

[75]Tertullian, *Apologeticus*, 50.

[76]From "A Service for Word and Table IV," *The United Methodist Hymbook* (Nashville: United Methodist Publishing House, 1989), 27.

51 NECESSITY AND LUXURY
Revelation 6:5–6

I looked, and there was a black horse!...And I heard what seemed to be a voice: "... A quart of wheat for a day's pay....but do not damage the olive oil and the wine!"

I heard it on the news: the drought in the midsection of this country, so disastrous for so many farmers, has resulted in a vintage year for grape-growers. My mind ran to a similar situation in the Book of Revelation: a scene where the black horse of famine comes to measure out in doles the precious grain, while at the same time indicating a plentitude of wine. Many Bible scholars believe that this reference found its origin in a situation during the reign of Domitian when there was a grain famine coupled with a bountiful grape harvest. Like the story out of Ohio in 1988, the wheat, corn, and barley failed during that year long ago, while the vineyards were overflowing. This produced then and produces now the strange situation of the shortage of a necessity and an abundance of a luxury.

When I thought about this in terms of the Lord's Supper, I was intrigued by the possibility that the bread that we share represents a necessity; the cup that we share represents a luxury. Is not the sacrifice of Christ for us like that? In Christ we find the necessities of life: such as faith and love. And we are also given the luxuries: such as joy and peace. When the old hymnwriter said Christ is our all in all, he spoke rightly. We come to this table, then, to remember and to celebrate all that Christ has done for us: the necessities and the luxuries of the community of faith. May we rejoice and dedicate ourselves to sharing this faith with others.

52   THE OTHER SIDE OF COMMUNION
Revelation 14:17–20; 19:17–21

... the angel swung his sickle over the earth and gathered the vintage of the earth, and he threw it into the great wine press of the wrath of God.... Come, gather for the great supper of God, to eat...the flesh of all, both free and slave, both small and great.

Toward the end of the Book of Revelation are two gory stories. In the first an angel swings his sickle over the earth and gathers the vintage of earth and throws "it"—that is to say, us—into the great wine press of the wrath of God. And it says that the blood will flow as high as a horse's bridle for two hundred miles. The second text has an angel go out to gather the flesh of all people, people of high and low estate, for the great banquet of God. The flesh is brought and the birds of midheaven have a grand feast, gorging themselves. Not a pretty picture.

I have not lost any sleep over these texts because, as with most of the horrible images in Revelation, they are not to be taken literally. But I do believe they should be taken seriously. These two images of flesh and blood remind us of a great truth that rests on the other side of communion. As Carlyle Marney said of Jesus, "The one who would save others cannot save himself."[77] And as Burton Mack has said of us, "We come to the table to take life in the absolute certainty that we will be taken."[78] The Revelation stories show in graphic form how God can turn the tables on a haughty humanity. We devour life daily. We need to remember that we can be devoured. We affirm at this table, in the face of that, that Jesus' death and ours can have meaning. Paraphrasing Pascal, "Man is the weakest reed in nature. Anything can kill him. But he knows why he dies."[79] Yes. We live and we die unto Christ and we seal that promise here at his table.

---

[77]Paraphrased from Marney, *The Crucible of Redemption*, 41-46.

[78]Burton Mack, from a lecture in AM 392, "Narratives in Mark," School of Theology at Claremont, Spring 1980.

[79]Paraphrased from Blaise Pascal, *Pensee's*, Section VI, No. 347.

Historical

HISTORICAL

53 LISTEN PLAINLY: I AM A CHRISTIAN

The cost of Christian discipleship can be very high. Many Christians down through the centuries have been called upon to lay down their lives for Christ. One of the better-known martyrs is the beloved Polycarp, bishop of Smyrna in the second century. He was hauled before the Roman proconsul and urged to curse Christ. Polycarp replied: "Eighty and six years I have served him, and he never did me any wrong. How can I blaspheme my King who saved me?" The proconsul kept on urging him to curse Christ. To which Polycarp finally replied, "Listen plainly: I am a Christian."

So they took him to be burned, and the account says that after Polycarp finished his prayer the men attending the fire lighted it.

> And when the flame flashed forth, we saw a miracle....For the fire made the shape of a vaulted chamber, like a ship's sail filled by the wind, and made a wall around the body of the martyr. And he was in the midst, not as burning flesh, but as bread baking or as gold and silver refined in a furnace. And we perceived such a sweet aroma as the breath of incense or some other precious spice.

> At length, when the lawless men saw that his body could not be consumed by the fire, they commanded an executioner...to stab him with a dagger. And when he did this a great quantity of blood came forth, so that the fire was quenched and the whole crowd marvelled....[1]

It is a remarkable story. Whether embellished by the eyes of faith or not, we do not know. What we do know is that even as the saints and martyrs died, other Christians came to see their deaths in tune with that of Jesus. The body and the blood, the bread and the cup, became more powerful than empires. It is still not easy to be a Christian. But we have in this table an assurance and a voice. We have the assurance that God is with us as God has been with God's people down through the ages. And we have a voice. When we come to the table, we say to the world, "Listen plainly: I am a Christian."

---

[1]"The Martyrdom of Polycarp, as told in the Letter of the Church of Smyrna to the Church of Philomelium," ed. Massey H. Shepherd, Jr., in *Early Christian Fathers*, Vol. I of the *Library of Christian Classics*, ed. Cyril C. Richardson (Philadelphia: Westminster, 1953), 152-155.

54 IT IS ENOUGH

There are no doubt people who wish there was more to our communion service—who wish there were more magical words, more bells and whistles, more ethereal music, more special lighting effects...to get us in the mood. But we don't do that; we simply gather, as we were commanded, to eat and drink in memory and in love.

There is a story out of the third century that may help us here. St. Anthony was a leader among the desert monastics, and the story says that three religious men used to go to visit him each year. Two of them would discuss their thoughts about the salvation of their souls with him, but the third always remained silent and did not ask him anything. After many years, Abba Anthony said to him, "You often come here to see me, but you never ask me anything," to which the other replied, "It is enough for me to see you, Father,"[2]

One of the great needs of our consumer-oriented society is a sense of "enough." And our time about this table is helpful there. It is enough for us to be here, to know of the sacrifice that brought us to this table and of the spiritual resources that are available to us here. We do not fancy up the service because we do not need fancying up ourselves— we need simplifying. We need the bread of life and the cup of salvation. And here they are. And it is enough.

---

[2]*The Sayings of the Desert Fathers*, tr. Benedicta Ward (London: A. R. Mowbray, 1975), 6.

55 EATING THE WORD OF GOD

Romanos the Melodist was the greatest poet-preacher of sixth-century Byzantium. Legend has it that one Christmas Eve he was keeping an allnight vigil in church when Mary, the mother of Jesus, appeared to him in a dream,

> ... and handing him a scroll of paper she commanded him to eat it. The holy man obediently opened his mouth and swallowed the paper. Upon awakening, he climbed into the pulpit and began to chant [his great poem-sermon on the Nativity].[3]

This concept is not as farfetched as it may sound to us. Today, having to "eat your words" implies rash predictions, embarrassment, and

---

[3]St. Nikodemas of Mount Athos, in Eva Catafygiotu Topping, "St. Romanos, Ikon of a Poet," *Greek Orthodox Theological Review*, 12:1 (1966), 92-93.

regret. Our ancestors, however, were so in touch with Scripture that they spoke of consuming it, like a hungry child, and deriving great spiritual nourishment. As Jeremiah said, "Your words were found, and I ate them, and your words became to me a joy and the delight of my heart" (Jeremiah 15:16).

The Gospel According to John tells us that "the Word became flesh" and dwelt among us in the person of Jesus Christ. At this table we commemorate the sacrifice of Jesus through these symbols of his body and blood. Jesus Christ *is* the Word of God. May this rich feast of God's Word become for us the joy and delight of our hearts.

56 SACRILEGE AND SUPERSTITION

We come now to the Lord's Table. Many of you have worshipped in churches where you come forward to kneel to receive communion and where the priest or minister actually places the communion wafer in your mouth. Did you ever wonder why it is done that way? As best I can tell, for two reasons, both of which may be traced to the Middle Ages. The church held the communion bread, the host, the body of Christ, in the highest reverence, and insisted that it not be profaned. Listen to this story from *The Chronicles of Thomas of Eccleston*:

> Behold! On that very Easter Day, when all the people communicated, a certain wicked and infamous man named Getius went to Communion, and having received without reverence, immediately went aside and sat upon a bench and began to gossip with those standing near, being no more concerned than if he had but a morsel of bread in his mouth, when lo! Brother Mansuetus beheld the Eucharist go forth from the man's mouth and fall to the ground some distance away. Immediately Brother Mansuetus went and told the priest, a man very venerable, what he had seen, who straightway commanded him to go and search for the Host where it had fallen. And, going to search for it, he immediately found it in exactly the same spot, though for a long time the people had been passing by that spot as they went up to receive communion and returned. The boy, therefore, with much reverence, received the said Host and all the consecrated Hosts which remained upon the altar, and was unspeakably confirmed in faith.[4]

The second reason for the care given to the Eucharist is that during this same period there were so many cults and superstitions around that the church was afraid people might take the bread home and put it to superstitious use. So, to stop that, they began putting it right in people's mouths, and they made it so that it would melt quickly.

---

[4]*The Chronicles of Thomas of Eccleston*, tr. Father Cuthbert, O.S.F.C. (St. Louis: B. Herder, 1909), 121-122.

I can appreciate the sensitive care and concern the medieval church demonstrated. The Lord's Supper is to be taken seriously. And we do today, though not magically so. We have a bite of bread and a little cup of juice to remind us of how Christ died for our sins, to inspire us to more Christlike living, to witness to the unity of Christ's church, and just to have a quiet time to think about these things. And, unlike the church of the Middle Ages, we hope you will take it with you—take this service and all it means home with you and hold onto it during the week. Come to the table. Take all you need. We have plenty.

57   TABLE OF PEACE

It is not easy to be Christian. It never has been. That was a heavy meal Jesus shared with his disciples that night. He told them he was leaving; he told them he was going to be betrayed—surely the disciples were stunned. But he did not leave them comfortless. He gave them this cup and this loaf, not just for remembrance, not just for anticipation, but to ease their present pain.

In the year 1522 the church at Wittenburg was falling apart. There was anger and hostility and fear. People were lost and confused. They did not know what to do or which way to go. Martin Luther stood up, and in the midst of their suffering he offered them the Lord's Supper. He spoke to them about the peace a Christian could find in communion, and he closed with these words: "For this bread is a comfort to the sorrowing, a healing for the sick, a life for the dying, a food for the hungry, and rich treasure for all the poor and needy."[5]

I wish I had said that, but I am glad that he did. For he has found us all in those few words, found us at our own level of weakness and pain. And for those of us who are sorrowing, sick, dying, hungry, poor, and needy, he holds out the Eucharist as comfort, healing, life, food, and treasure. There is a blessing for every need here. How good it is to come to this table, even if just for a minute, to receive the peace of God that the world of its own accord cannot give.

---

[5]Martin Luther, "The Sixth Sermon, March 14, 1522, Friday after Invocavit" *Luther's Works*, ed. & trans. John W. Doberstein (Philadelphia: Fortress, 1959), 51:95.

58 LAST SUPPER

Friedrich Schleiermacher (1768-1834) has been called the father of modern theology. But he was more than a great thinker; he was also a person of profound faith. And nothing exemplified this life of faith more than the manner of his leaving it.

> His [last] ailment developed inflammation of the lungs, and after a week of intense suffering, the great, brave, tender spirit passed away. His wife, in her notes of that week, relates that after the death film had already overspread his eyes, and his whole aspect was that of death, he suddenly raised himself, and in a clear and strong voice spoke out, "I have never clung to the dead letter; and we have the atoning death of Jesus Christ, His body and blood." He then desired the things necessary for Communion to be quickly brought, and after solemn prayer, administered it to each of those present, while an expression of heavenly rapture spread over his features, and a strange lustre shone in his eyes. Finally he himself partook adding, "On these words of Scripture I rely; they are the foundation of my faith"; and after pronouncing the blessing, sank back on his pillow with a farewell word and look of love, and in a few minutes breathed his last, February 12th, 1834.[6]

On these words of Scripture we too rely: "This is my body, broken for you." We will live by them and, when the time comes, we will die by them as well.

---

[6]*Selected Sermons of Schleiermacher*, trans. Mary F. Wilson (New York: Funk and Wagnalls, 1890), 37.

59 THE LORD'S SUPPER AS SYMBOL

John Meredith Trible (1851-1891) was a gifted young pastor/ teacher of the nineteenth century. He was professor of biblical literature and vice-president of Bethany College, as well as pastor of the campus church, at his untimely death. Of him it was said that "his addresses at the table of the Lord…bore the mark of genius."[7] He once responded to all, including Luther, who argued for the literal presence of Christ in the elements of the Lord's Supper with this story:

> When this beautiful building in which we gather today was being planned, one of the brethren…brought the plans around for my inspection, saying, as he held up a roll of broad sheets before me, "This

---

[7]Archibald McLean, "Biographical Sketch" in *Trible's Sermons* (St. Louis: Christian Publishing, 1892), 9.

is our new church." I am not bright in matters of architecture. But I understood him. I did not suppose that he had the new church done up in a paper package and carrying it around in his buggy or under his arm; that he was about to spread the whole building out on my lap....I knew that he was speaking figuratively, and meant that this is a likeness of the church; this represents the church. And yet when we come to interpret the Scriptures we cast away all our common sense and begin to grow red in the face if anyone seeks to gainsay us, reiterating that "it means what it says and it says what it means," and that any other view of it is a perversion of the plain word of Scripture. Is it not plain, then, that the Lord's Supper is not a communication to us of the literal body and blood of Christ, but a communication of the redeeming love which was manifest in the breaking of that body and the shedding of that blood? "Do this, as oft as ye do it, in remembrance of me."[8]

This is as clear an exposition of this approach to the table as I have encountered. Rich in symbol, rich in meaning, rich in love is the table spread before us. Let us be grateful as we partake.

---

[8]J. M. Trible, "The Significance of the Lord's Supper," *Ibid.*, 256-257.

60 THE LORD'S SUPPER AS SPIRITUAL REALITY

The story of Frederick William Robertson (1816-1853) is one of the most remarkable in the history of preaching. All but unknown during his short life as an English pastor, his influence upon preaching grew after his death until he would be called "the most influential preacher in the English-speaking world."[9] His approach to understanding the Eucharist is instructive:

In opposition to the dissenting view, it *is* Christ's body and blood received; in opposition to the Romanist's view, it *is not* Christ's body and blood to those who receive it unworthily. We do not go between the two. Each of these opposite statements of the Dissenter or of the Roman Catholic are truths, and we retain them. It is not merely bread and wine; it is, spiritually, Christ's body and blood: God present spiritually, not materially, to those who receive it worthily—i.e., to the faithful. It is not Christ's body and blood to those on whose feelings and conduct it does not tell.[10]

Robertson is suggesting here that what we have at the table is neither transubstantiation nor symbol; it is spiritual reality. He further sug-

---

[9]A. W. Blackwood, "Introduction" to James R. Blackwood, *The Soul of Frederick W. Robertson* (New York: Harper & Bros., 1947), ix.

[10]*Life, Letters, Lectures and Addresses of Frederick W. Robertson,* ed. Stopford Brooke (New York: Harper & Bros., 1870), 316.

gests that the critical question is not the nature of the stuff on the table, but the effect it has upon those who partake. To those who are faithful, to those who are moved by receiving the elements and show that by how they live their lives, this is the body and blood of Christ.

Here we have with the Sacrament the same problem we face concerning the Word of God. Is its meaning and power dependent upon the response of those who receive it? Robertson said yes. So did St. Paul. The argument is strong. And while I am nervous about any understanding that makes divine reality dependent upon human action, I am not afraid to say that our approach to the table is one of the determinative factors in shaping what happens there.

61 PASSING OVER

"Christ our passover is sacrificed for us. Therefore let us keep the feast, not with the old leaven of malice and wickedness; but with the unleavened bread of sincerity and truth." (1 Cor. 5:7b–8, KJV)

Scots pastor Richard Waterson, reflecting on the Lord's Supper, told this story just a century ago. It seems that once, some centuries before, the city of Rotterdam was under attack by the Duke of Galva. Most of the inhabitants made a gallant but unsuccessful resistance by fighting for their lives within their barricaded houses. In one house, however, the people had a different plan. They killed a goat, splashed the door and entryway with its blood, and then left the door wide open to the invading force. Thinking that in that house vengeance had already done its worst, and that these were the bloody tokens of a completed massacre, the troops of the Duke passed by. The house is called "the house of a thousand terrors," in memory of the feelings of the trembling company in the upper room as they waited to see whether or not their ruse would work and they be spared.[11]

This is a strange kind of sanctuary, neither the first nor the last time the passover motif has been baptized for Christian use. I would not for a moment have denied those huddling folk their chance for survival. What leaves me uneasy is the use that has been made of their story. Many people wear the cross of Christ around their necks as a kind of amulet to ward off evil. The bloody sacrifice of Christ commemorated at the table is trivialized when we partake of the elements prophylactically. The loaf and cup do not inoculate us against evil. Rather, they help us to see evil for what it really is: powerful enough to kill the beloved Jesus, but not strong enough to overcome the resurrecting power of God. Christ our passover is sacrificed for us. Christ our Lord reigns forever.

---

[11]Richard Waterson, *Thoughts on the Lord's Supper* (Edinburgh: Andrew Eliot, 1892), 63.

62   CRUST OF BREAD

One of my heroes is mountaineer and naturalist John Muir (1838-1914). I read his books and thrill to his beautiful perceptions of the natural world. Writing of his adventures, he often described mountain interludes in this way: "I ate my crust of bread on the summit..." Muir lived and ate simply. He would take what he called his "crust of bread" (a small loaf, I assume) with him on his climbs. When he reached the summit he would eat the bread and survey the panorama that spread before him in every direction. I further assume that the bread thus became for him both reward for the climb and energy for the return to civilization.

This service is like that. We have come a long way in our spiritual journey. So rest here a spell, eat your crust of bread, and remember. Survey the past, present, and especially the future that spreads out before you. We still have a long way to go in fulfilling the task to which we have been called. So be energized in Christ for the mission in front of us. Rest. Give thanks. Remember. Walk on.

63   THROUGHOUT ALL AGES...

The greatest study on the history of the Eucharist is doubtless that of the Benedictine monk Dom Gregory Dix: *The Shape of the Liturgy*. Written a half-century ago, the book traces the origins and development of the Sacrament through a detailed 750 pages. Dix closes by pointing to the future, calling his last chapter "Throughout All Ages, World Without End."

I have never seen a more beautiful description of the impact this simple meal has had upon human history than the following paragraph from that chapter. It is here reproduced that readers of this book may have the chance to be touched as I was, and perhaps be moved to obtain and read the whole. Jesus took bread and, after giving thanks, broke it and gave it to them, saying "This is my body, broken for you. Do this, in remembrance of me":

> Was ever another command so obeyed? For century after century, spreading slowly to every continent and country and among every race on earth, this action has been done, in every conceivable human circumstance, for every conceivable human need from infancy and before it to extreme old age and after it, from the pinnacles of earthly greatness to the refuge of fugitives in the caves and dens of the earth. Men have found no better thing than this to do for kings at their crown-

ing and for criminals going to the scaffold; for armies in triumph or for a bride and bridegroom in a little country church; for the proclamation of a dogma or for a good crop of wheat; for the wisdom of the Parliament of a mighty nation or for a sick old woman afraid to die; for a schoolboy sitting an examination or for Columbus setting out to discover America; for the famine of whole provinces or for the soul of a dead lover; in thankfulness because my father did not die from pneumonia; for a village headman tempted to return to fetich because the yams have failed; because the Turk was at the gates of Vienna; for the repentence of Margaret; for the settlement of a strike; for a son for a barren woman; for Captain So-and-so, wounded and prisoner of war; when the lions roared in the nearby amphitheater; on the beach at Dunkirk; while the hiss of scythes in the thick June grass came faintly through the windows of the church; tremulously, by an old monk on the fiftieth anniversay of his vows; furtively, by an exiled bishop who had hewn timber all day in a prison camp near Murmansk; gorgeously, for the canonisation of St. Joan of Arc—one could fill many pages with the reasons why men have done this, and not tell a hundredth part of them. And best of all, week by week and month by month, on a hundred thousand successive Sundays, faithfully, unfailingly, across all the parishes of christendom, the pastors have done this just to *make* the *plebs sancta Dei*—the holy common people of God.[12]

---

[12]Dom Gregory Dix, *The Shape of the Liturgy* (London: A & C Black Ltd., 1945), 744. Used with permission. Dix wrote from the Anglo-European perspective of a half-century ago. We would write it differently today. But I doubt whether we would write it as well.

Literary

LITERARY

64 THE LEAST WE CAN DO

Before Leon Uris wrote his famous novel *Exodus*, he wrote another little book called *The Angry Hills*. In the story a group of British soldiers have been captured by the Germans in Greece during World War II. They have been herded into cattle cars and railroaded across Greece toward concentration camps. The prisoners are cramped and cold and hungry when the train reaches the poor little town of Kalamai. The train stops and the prisoners are removed from the cars to stretch, at which point this scene takes place:

> Crowds of Greeks gathered around the depot and wailed. The guards stretched out in an angry line to keep them separated from the prisoners.
>
> A little girl pushed past the guards and walked toward Mike and Soutar's group. She held a loaf of bread in her hands. A guard curtly ordered her to stop. The British yelled for the girl to go back. She kept coming, the bread outstretched for the hungry soldiers. Another order to halt…she moved on. The guard lowered his rifle.
>
> Soutar grabbed Mike's arm to control him. "Turn your head, don't look." Mike flinched as the shot echoed through the depot. British soldiers in screaming anger broke for the guard. Bayonets and clubs smashed them back into line. The loaf of bread rolled to a stop at Mike's feet. Soutar picked it up. "The least we can do is eat it," he said.[1]

Maybe someday there will be peace and reason in the world. Maybe someday we will be all that we can be. Maybe someday we will be able to sit down and share with Jesus the bread of our own life and sacrifice, the cup of our own redemption. Until that day we have the bread and cup that he gave us; we have the good and compelling news in them that he emptied himself for us. For I have received from the Lord that which I also deliver unto you, that in the same night in which he was betrayed, Jesus gave us this bread. The least we can do is eat it.

---

[1] Leon Uris, *The Angry Hills* (New York: Signet, 1955), 61.

65 LOVE IN ACTION

In *The Brothers Karamazov* Dostoevsky has the Elder say these words:

> Love in action is different from love in dreams. Love in dreams is beautiful and immediate, but active love requires persistence and hard work and sacrifice. Yet I predict that just when you see with horror that in spite of all your efforts you are getting farther from your goal instead of nearer to it—at that moment I predict that you will reach it and behold clearly the miraculous power of the Lord who has been all the time loving and mysteriously guiding you.[2]

There is a song that says, "Love came down at Christmas; love all lovely, love divine. Love was born at Christmas, star and angels gave the sign."[3] However, lest we forget, the coming of Christ was more than a dream of love, it was active love; it involved persistence, hard work, and sacrifice. We remember that at this table. And it is here that we know of a certainty that however far it may seem we are from our goal, God is ever near and will not let us go.

---

[2] Adapted from Fyodor Dostoevsky, *The Brothers Karamazov* (New York: W. W. Norton & Co., 1976), 49-50.

[3] "Love Came Down at Christmas," words: Christina Rossetti, music: trad. Irish melody, harm. David Evans.

66 HOW COULD I NOT BE AMONG YOU?

Ted Rosenthal was a young poet dying of cancer. Before his death he went to the wilderness to build a cabin, think, and write down his thoughts. These were collected in a magnificent little book called *How Could I Not Be Among You?* In it he encourages us to live, to dance, to run up mountains, to splash in the ocean. He concludes his last poem like this:

> Step lightly, we're walking home now.
> The clouds take every shape.
> We climb up the boulders; there is no plateau.
> We cross the stream and walk up the slope.
> See, the hawk is diving.
> The plain stretches out ahead, then the hills,
>   the valleys, the meadows.
> Keep moving people. How could I not be among you?[4]

---

[4] Ted Rosenthal, *How Could I Not Be Among You?* (New York: George Braziller, 1973), 74.

Look at the last line. There is a double-double meaning there that haunts me. Are we to keep moving ourselves or keep moving others or both? Was he bewailing the fact that he would not be among us to share the ongoing joys of life or was he somehow affirming that he would indeed be with us? I am not sure, but my guess is that Rosenthal intended both meanings both times, and that his last words give us a clue to the mystery of life and death as he experienced it.

Is this not also the mystery of the Lord's Table? We celebrate an absence *and* a presence. He is gone but he is here. Here we know the joy of sacrificial love and the sadness of separation. I have a dear friend who has trouble saying the words of institution for the Lord's Supper. His joy that Christ loved us so much and his sadness that the winsome Jesus had to die in such pain and leave us causes him to overflow in tears. If coming to the table makes you happy, that is as it should be. If coming to the table makes you sad, that is as it should be. But do come. Experience both the suffering and salvation that are at the heart of the gospel, a gospel that will make you so happy...that you could cry.

67 LIFE'S INK

Cuban poet Armando F. Valladares Perez was imprisoned in 1960 at the age of 23. In 1983, at the age of 45, he was finally released.

Despite torture, solitary confinement, and other punishment intended to silence him, Valladares continued to write. In a poem entitled, "The Best Ink," he wrote: "They have taken everything away from me/pens/pencils/ink/because they do not want me to write/but I still have life's ink/my own blood/and with it I can still write poems.[5]

It is not usual to think of blood as ink. But Valladares was right. What powerful ink it is! Jesus never wrote a book; he did not even leave us a manuscript. He gave us instead his own blood, his life's ink. Revitalized by the elements of this table, let us write that book and advance the reign of God with our lives and our faith.

---

[5]Emilie Trautmann, "Cuban poet freed after 22 years," *Matchbox*, published by Amnesty International USA (February 1983), 1.

68   THE FAILURE OF BREAD AND WINE

There is a good Italian novel by Ignazio Silone which is titled, in English, *Bread and Wine*. Published during the rise of Fascism, the book is a bittersweet commentary on human beings caught in the crunch between bureaucracy and radicalism. The bread and wine of the title refer to human love, which Silone sees as the only hope for those caught and mangled by political machinery. But the bread and wine fail.

The beloved old priest Don Benedetto is killed by poison wine in the chalice as he says mass.[6] Another character, lamenting the ways of young people, says,

> There comes a time when young people find the bread and wine of their own homes insipid. They look elsewhere for their nourishment. The bread and wine of the inns, which they find at the crossroads, on the highways, can alone appease their hunger and their thirst. But (people) cannot spend all of their time in inns.[7]

I thought, as I read, of the prodigal, swallowing his pride and coming home. I thought of John the Baptist, having given his all and yet still wondering at the end, "Are you the one who is to come or shall we look for another?" (Luke 7:19). One emerges from Silone's book with the feeling that, although love has failed, has been smashed by the principalities and powers, there remains somehow a victory, a victory of the human spirit. And one returns home to this table, after being satiated with the rich food of riotous living and the husks and pods of despair, because this minimalist feast, in memory of another who was smashed by the principalities and powers, speaks to us finally not of failure but of victory, the victory of the Holy Spirit. Come to the table, to partake of the bread and wine of home.

---

[6]Ignazio Silone, *Bread and Wine*, tr. Gwenda David and Eric Mosbacher (New York: Harper, 1937), 278-279.
[7]*Ibid.*, 150.

69   NIGHT WITH EBON PINION

One of my favorite hymns is fast disappearing from modern hymnbooks. It is called "Night with Ebon Pinion," and I suppose what first attracted me to it was its relentless beat (more suited to drums than piano!) and its interesting title. What is "ebon pinion"? "Black feather." But why a hymn about black feathers?

Night with ebon pinion, brooded o'er the vale;
All around was silent, save the night-wind's wail,
When Christ, the Man of sorrows, in tears, and sweat, and blood,
Prostrate in the garden, raised His voice to God.[8]

Think about it. How dark a black-feathered bird would be at night! And how frightful would be a night that came winging on black feathers, a night that a James Weldon Johnson might describe as "blacker than a thousand midnights down in a cypress swamp."[9] That was the kind of night Jesus spent in the garden: the dark night of the soul, when darkness came on brooding black wings and surrounded him. And yet, in Tennyson's words:

We have a power in the night,
Which made the darkness and the light,
And dwells not in the light alone.[10]

When we remember how Jesus gave himself for us, we cannot help but feel saddened by the suffering and sadness of that night. Our souls, too, have dark nights, nights when we feel lost and alone. But we need to remember that we have a power that dwells not in the light alone. So that wherever we go, however dark it becomes, we can know that God is with us, and that Jesus has gone before us. If we will have faith, then, as it says in Revelation (22:5), the day will come when we need no light or lamp, because the Lord God will be our light, and the blackwinged bird will fly away. Come to the table in remembrance of the Man of Sorrows, who is the Light of the world.

---

[8]"Night with Ebon Pinion," words: Love H. Jameson, music: Joseph P. Powell.
[9]James Weldon Johnson, *God's Trombones* (New York: Viking, 1927), 17.
[10]Alfred, Lord Tennyson, in Hughell E. W. Fosbroke, *By Means of Death* (Greenwich, CT: Seabury, 1956), 61.

70   STOLEN BREAD OR GIFT FROM GOD?

Two stories from the novels of Nikos Kazantzakis offer interesting perspectives on the Eucharist. In *The Greek Passion* a starving group of exiles is camped on a mountain overlooking a village rich with food. Finally, one night a group of men make their way down to the village to steal food. A ladder is there leading to the storehouses of the richest man in town. They help themselves to the corn, oil, and wine. The next morning the rich man sees the ladder and checks his storehouses, but everything is in order. "Luckily no thieves came," he says.

But when the refugees awaken on the mountain, there sits the food before them. Kazantzakis describes what happened then:

> News of the miracle spread...four angels, during the night, had brought
> corn, oil and wine to the starving. The simple among them believed
> and crossed themselves. The more shrewd glanced with smiles at
> Yannakos and Loukas (two of the "thieves"). The women fell upon the
> corn and at once began to sift it, singing softly as though to lull a baby
> to sleep, as though they were dandling the Child Jesus....In a twin-
> kling they crushed a certain quantity on the stones, fashioned a flat
> cake and baked it on the embers, moistening it with a little oil to make
> it more tasty; then they gave everyone a mouthful, sharing it out like
> the consecrated bread; and straightaway they felt comforted in flesh
> and blood, as though that bread were really the Body of Christ. After
> that, all drank a drop of wine, and the women could not keep back
> their tears. "O God," they sighed, "a mouthful of bread, a sip of wine—
> that's all that's needed to make the soul feel it's growing wings."[11]

The "thieves" thought they had taken the victuals when, in fact, they
had somehow been gifted with them. They thought they had done it
themselves, while in truth they had not. That is often the position we
find ourselves in at this table. We make our prayers like the father did at
the dinner table in the old movie *Shenandoah:* "We cleared and plowed
the fields, we planted the seed, we harvested the grain, we made the
bread, but we thank you anyway, God. Amen." We prepared this table,
we paid for the elements. Like the "thieves" in *The Greek Passion*, we
think we did it ourselves. This is a good time to remember that, if we
think that, we are wrong. We have not earned or merited the grace that
flows from this table. In truth it comes to us as a dearly puchased gift, a
gift from Christ.

The second story is from *The Fratricides*. Father Yanaros, a good
man, is trying to keep his village together during the difficult days of
the Greek civil war. One day a monk comes to town, his donkey laden
with gifts he has received from other villages. He claims to have a sacred relic, a sash worn by the Virgin Mary herself, and he invites the
people to come and bring their gifts to offer to the Virgin. The village
priest is tired of seeing his poor people made poorer by such scams and
the following scene unfolds:

> Father Yanaros turned and looked at the crowd, and his heart
> twisted with pain. "My children," he said, "pray before the Holy Sash,
> but do not give a grain of wheat to the monk. You are poor, you are
> hungry; your children are starving; the Virgin has no need of offer-
> ings. That She should take from you? God forbid! She gives to you!
> Why do they call Her Mother of Christianity? Would She watch her
> children starve and not reach out a compassionate hand to give them a
> piece of bread? This holy man here, who came to our village to fill his
> baskets and depart, saw our poverty. He looked at the hungry children
> who ran behind him, and his heart ached. Is he not a faithful servant of

---

[11]Kazantzakis, *The Greek Passion*, tr. Jonathan Griffin (New York: Simon and
Schuster, 1953), 378.

the Virgin? Does the Virgin Mother not dwell within his heart? What need has he of food and luxuries? Many years ago he turned his back upon the riches of this futile life and went to Mount Athos to become sanctified. And now he feels compassion at our disaster and has reached a decision, God bless him. He is going to distribute among us everything that he has gathered from the villages he passed to get here. Everything in his baskets![12]

The crowd cheered, the baskets were emptied, and the fat monk looked at Father Yanaros with poison in his eyes. The priest said to the monk, "There is no greater joy than in giving bread to the hungry." But the monk was not joyful. The first story speaks of stolen bread that was, in fact, a gift. This one speaks of bread also gained under "false" pretenses, bread grudgingly given that the people think is a gift. This is more difficult. Can "grudge bread" be holy? Put in a slightly different way, can we come to the table in what Paul calls "an unworthy manner" or eat bread placed before us unworthily and still be blessed by the partaking? I hope Paul will forgive me for saying "yes." I believe that no matter how we or the bread got to the table, there can be blessing in the sharing, even when we do not feel worthy, even when we are not "in the mood," even when we do not expect it.

Fred Craddock tells a story about some college boys who get drunk. One of them has a talent for mimicking revival preachers so, as they pass a sanctuary, they go in and the mimic climbs into the pulpit and begins to "preach," egged on by the "amens" and "hallelujahs" of his comrades. It just so happens that a custodian, cleaning the room, stops to listen and, not knowing that he is listening to a charade, "gets saved." Well, is he really saved? "Yes," Craddock rightly answers.[13] God can work through even false prophets. Stolen bread and grudge bread can be vehicles of grace. And we, sinners that we are, grudging though we may serve, can still be blessed by God and useful friends of Christ. Come to the table and receive the blessings of God.

---

[12]Kazantzakis, *The Fratricides*, 30-31.
[13]I have this story of Craddock's sermon from Gilbert Davis.

71 SWILL

In Trevanian's novel, *The Summer of Katya,* is this disturbing passage:

> The waiter brought his wine. "Ah," he said, draining the glass then shuddering with a grimace. "It's sometimes difficult to recall that, with the benefit of a few incantations, this swill can become the blood of Christ."[14]

I have never particularly cared for communion by intinction, or dipping. Bread is wonderful. Wine or juice is wonderful. Bread dipped in juice is purple goop. Once I served at a table where one thousand people came forward to dip bread into the chalice. By the time they were finished, the cup *did* look like swill.

I like my rituals nice, neat, clean, no bread contaminated with juice and vice-versa, no body with blood all over it. But the Eucharist does not work that way. It is very messy. And confusing. Why did Jesus have to die? Why was his body broken, his blood spilled? Was there no other way? If the theory of atonement leaves us with a God who sent Jesus to die, what does that say about God? Jesus died on the cross in agony. Part of our agony lies in our struggle with the meaning of the cross.

Some might wish there were some incantations that would make easy sense of the cross and the Eucharist. But there are not. There is simply this: While we were yet sinners, Christ died for us. Strange and messy as that is, it is the very foundation of our life and hope.

---

[14]Trevanian, *The Summer of Katya* (New York: Ballantine, 1983), 132. This meditation is perhaps best reserved for colloquies or seminars, rather than public worship. Some people may find the language offensive. Words like "swill" and "goop" may be button-pressers, which might cause people to ignore (or not hear) the point of the meditation because of their antipathy to the language.

72 LAMENT FOR A SON

Lament for a Son is a little book by Nicholas Wolterstorff, written after the tragic death of his son Eric in a mountain-climbing accident. At one point Wolterstorff writes:

> It was late at night when I returned home, but I assembled the family. I remember only what I said first and last. "Our Eric is gone," I said. And at the end, that we must learn to live as faithfully and authentically with Eric gone as we had tried to do with Eric present.

How do we do that? And what does it mean? It will take a long time to learn.

It means not forgetting him. It means speaking of him. It means remembering him. *Remembering:* one of the profoundest features of the Christian and Jewish way of being-in-the-world and being-in-history is remembering. "Remember," "do not forget," "do this as a remembrance." We are to hold the past in remembrance and not let it slide away. For in history we find God.[15]

Wolterstorff is right. In history we find God. And how fortunate we are that this is true, that God has chosen to meet us in history, not outside it. Supremely, God meets us in Jesus, who also died tragically. We have "assembled the family" around this table to remember his death. We also remember that Eric's hope and ours is found in the great eternal truth that Jesus' death was not the end, but the beginning: the beginning of a new age and a new world. Eat, drink, remember, look forward, and love God.

---

[15]Nicholas Wolterstorff, *Lament for a Son* (Grand Rapids, MI: Eerdmans, 1987), 28.

73   'TWIXT THE CUP AND THE LIP

Life is filled with "betwixts and betweens," even in worship. Medieval writers would talk about what happened "between the apse and the ambo" of a church. Further back, the prophet Joel advised the priests to make their prayers "between the vestibule and the altar" and God would send food to the hungry people (2:17-19). Further back still is the ancient proverb, sometimes attributed to Homer, which goes like this: "There is many a slip, 'twixt the cup and the lip."[16] I think that the point of all this is that one would be surprised how much can happen in a very small space in a very short time, and under very mundane circumstances.

There were five thousand hungry people before him. And in the short time between Jesus' breaking of the few loaves of bread and his feeding of the people, something extraordinary happened. A multiplication took place. Consider again the phrase: "'twixt the cup and the lip." How much can happen from the time you pick up a cup until the time you drink what is in it? The answer is: something extraordinary if the cup is a communion cup. Many times I have picked up the cup with a ho-hum attitude, and suddenly some thought would cross my mind, and the drinking would become meaningful. Wherever you are right now, may the

---

[16]See Palladas, *Greek Anthology*, Book X, Epigram 32.

significance of what we are about to do…recreate once again the pivotal moment of the church, when Jesus took bread and wine and blessed them. This is the moment when the church is born and reborn, and we are at one with all people everywhere who gather about the Lord's table. May this meaning transform the ordinary into the extraordinary for you, 'twixt the cup and the lip.

74 THREE CHAIRS

In Thoreau's description of his little hut at Walden Pond, he said that he had three chairs there: one for solitude, one for friendship, and one for society.[17] Our gathering about the Lord's Table is very similar. We have one chair for solitude. Whitehead said once that religion is what we do with our "solitariness."[18] This is the place where we can meet our Savior face to face, to partake in quietness of the elements of personal grace.

We have one chair for friendship. To gather as a group of friends to share the loaf and cup is a moving experience. To pass the elements to each person in turn: "The body of Christ, broken for you, my friend; the blood of Christ, the cup of salvation, for you." Disagreements and misunderstandings can fall away when we meet each other under the judgment of his love.

We have one chair for society, the affectionate world-wide society of Jesus Christ, all those in all places, who take the loaf and cup in remembrance of him and in dedication to the cause for which he lived and died. All three chairs are close by the table this morning. You are welcome to "sit" in the one most appropriate for you.

---

[17]Henry David Thoreau, *Walden* (New York: Grosset and Dunlap, 1910), 184.

[18]Alfred North Whitehead, *Religion in the Making* (New York: New American Library, 1974), 16.

75 TRUSTING THE RESULT WOULD BE BREAD

I suppose we are spoiled at the church where I worship. People in our congregation bake the bread for communion (a practice made easier by the advent of bread machines). There is a catch, however, that became evident to me last Sunday. We returned to our seats from the table where we had partaken. I leaned over to my son and whispered, "That was good bread!" I immediately felt a bit guilty. Here I was, supposed to be thinking about Jesus and instead reflecting on how wonderful the bread was. My thoughts were never so interrupted by the wafers and chunks we used to have.

But I went with the thought: good bread. We here take it for granted, like clean water, healthy food, and so forth. I know that many in this world would rejoice in my problem: being distracted by good bread. Then I recalled a story from John Muir, the naturalist, and looked it up when I got home. Writing about his first summer in the Sierra in 1868, he said:

> I had to make as well as earn my daily bread, both of which operations were attended with difficulty. I filled the big cylindrical pot with dough and applied hot coals on the hearth, trusting the result would be bread. But the sticky compost, innocent of yeast or any patent inflating mixture, remained as passive beneath the fire as a martyr, and upon being pried out of the pot next morning was found to be black...and perfectly solid. It became extremely hard in cooling and, on attempting to cut out a section of it with a butcher knife it broke with a glassy fracture, and I began to hope that like Goodyear I had discovered a new article of manufacture. My teeth were good, and I rasped on a block of it like a squirrel on a nut. I told my troubles to a neighboring shepherd, and he made me wise about sour-dough ferment, and henceforth my bread was good.[19]

I decided by the end of the service that the thought was all right, even important. Good bread has often been dearly achieved in human history. So has good faith. We take this good bread in gratitude for the one who baked it and in enormous gratitude for the one whose love and sacrifice are the basis for our faith. And we take it trusting that it will remind us of that one, whom we call the bread of life—the good bread of life.

---

[19]John Muir, *John of the Mountains*, ed. Linnie Marsh Wolfe (Madison: Univ. of Wisconsin, 1979), 5.

76   A BILLION GALLONS?

In Richard Ellison's classic searing novel of rising black consciousness called *Invisible Man*, there is a powerful scene where two black leaders who have chosen different ways confront each other. Ras the Exhorter seeks to shame the young man who has chosen to work together with whites instead of against them:

> Why you with these white folks? Why?...He got you so you don't trust your black intelligence? You young, don't play you'self cheap, mahn. It took a billion gallons of black blood to make you![20]

The line stopped me. How much blood? A billion gallons? And how much blood did it take to make us Christian? Do we need our consciousness raised in this regard? First there was the sorrow and love that flowed mingled down from the cross; then the blood of the martyrs, the saints, the servants, the evangelizers, the builders, the faithful ones, on and on. So many gallons.

Eugene Lowry tells about a parsonage being built on the other side of the cemetery from a church.[21] In the excavation they unearthed bones, which research told them were slave bones from the period before the War Between the States. Hearing this later from the pastor as they sat in the study of the parsonage, Lowry asked, "How could one prepare a sermon, fix dinner, even sleep...with all those bones just a few feet below?" Then he answered his own question: "We all do."

Yes. Our lives and our work are held up by so many bones, so much blood. Our time at the table today is a good time to remember that, to confess our sin, pray for forgiveness, and thank God for the mercy of the gospel.

---

[20]Ralph Ellison, *Invisible Man* (New York: Vintage Books, 1972), 361, 364.
[21]Eugene Lowry, sermon preached at the annual meeting of the Academy of Homiletics, Pasadena, California, 6 Dec. 1991.

77   THE GAUNTLET WITH A GIFT IN IT

In medieval times to throw down a gauntlet (protective glove) was to issue a challenge. The act is long gone, but the phrase remains. And the communion meal throws down a spiritual gauntlet in front of us time and again. There is plenty in this supper to challenge us, to call us from our lethargy to follow the one who laid down his life for us. But it is not just a challenge. Listen to these lines from Elizabeth Barrett Browning:

God answers sharp and sudden on some prayers,
And thrusts the thing we have prayed for in our face,
A gauntlet with a gift in 't.[22]

We pray to become more Christlike, to be better followers of Jesus. And sometimes that prayer is answered with a gauntlet: "You want to follow Jesus? Then take up your cross and walk." When the challenge seems overwhelming, it may help to remember that this is a gauntlet with a gift in it. God "tempers the wind" to us as we stand shorn and sinful before the table. And the gift is grace. Knowing that, in spite of everything, when the cross is too heavy, when we stumble and fall under the load, God loves us still, wants the best for us, and will not let us go. When the implications of the supper threaten to undo us, remember that God loves us beyond our imagining and gifts us beyond our dreams with overflowing grace. Take bread. Take wine. Take heart.

---

[22]Elizabeth Barrett Browning, in Paul E. Sherer, "A Gauntlet with a Gift in It," *Interpretation* 20:4 (October 1966), 387 ff.

78 BREAD AND CIRCUSES

Jim Murray is one of America's most beloved sportswriters. He closes his autobiography with these words:

> The ancient Romans described the secret of successful rule as "Bread and Circuses." I covered the Circus. I felt privileged to have done so. Some of the happiest hours of my life were spent in a press box. Sure, I helped keep the hype going, the calliope playing. I can live with that. It's what I am.[23]

As I read those words, I paused and thought. Unlike Murray, I covered the Bread. I have spent much of my life seeking out and trying to understand and interpret the presence of God among us. Nowhere is that presence more palpable than at the table. In many ways God's presence is still a mystery, felt but not understood. I can live with that. I also must work with it. We stand in wonder at the intersection of sacred and secular. The spiritual hunger of many, the physical hunger of many others: How are they related? This is my body. Feed my sheep. Powerful stuff. It is a privilege to be here.

---

[23]Jim Murray, *Jim Murray: An Autobiography* (New York: Macmillan, 1993), 262.

79 I'D LIKE HIM NOT TO BE FORGOTTEN

A half-century ago Lenore Coffee and her husband wrote a play called *Family Portrait*. The family is that of Jesus, and the play depicts their reactions to the events of his ministry, although Jesus himself is never seen on stage. The play ran for a long time in New York and one of its most haunting moments comes in the closing scene. It is an evening or so after the crucifixion. Mary and Jesus' younger brother, Judah, are alone on the stage in their Nazareth home. Judah's wife, Deborah, is upstairs with a midwife, expecting a baby momentarily.

MARY. If the baby's a boy—what are you going to name him?

JUDAH. We haven't decided.

MARY. I wish— (She pauses.)

JUDAH. What, mother?

MARY. Will you do something for me, Judah?

JUDAH. Of course I will! What is it?

BEULAH. (From upstairs) Judah!

JUDAH. (Calling up) Coming! (He starts up two or three steps, Mary going a step or two with him. He stops—)

MARY. (Looking up as she speaks) If it's a boy, will you name him after your brother—(Hesitantly)—After Jesus, I mean?

JUDAH. Why—why, yes, Mother. I'll talk to Deborah about it—(He leans over the railing of the staircase and kisses her. Mary, now alone, turns and walks toward the table. She picks up a taper and begins to light the seven-branched candlesticks.)

MARY. It's a nice name—(Pause) I'd like him not to be forgotten—

(THE CURTAIN FALLS)[24]

He hasn't been, Mary. He didn't need a nephew named after him to stave off for a little while the creeping ravages of time. He lives. He loves. He reigns with God and the Holy Spirit, world without end. And every time we come to this table, every time we grow in understanding of who God would have us be and how God would have us live, we remember Jesus and give thanks to God for his saving presence among us.[25]

---

[24]Lenore Coffee and William Joyce Owen, *Family Portrait* (New York: Samuel French, 1940), 129.
[25]I owe my knowledge of this play and most of the ideas in this meditation to Hunter Beckelhymer.

Seasonal

SEASONAL

ADVENT I

80 IN ANTICIPATION OF HIM
Matthew 26:26–29

"I tell you, I will never again drink of this fruit of the vine until that day when I drink it new with you in my Father's kingdom."

In Matthew's version of the Lord's Supper, Jesus broke the bread, offered the cup, and then said this: "I tell you, I will never again drink of this fruit of the vine until that day when I drink it new with you in my Father's kingdom." What is different here? There is no hint (as in Luke and 1 Corinthians) that this is a memorial feast, something to be done "in remembrance of him." The emphasis is not upon the past, but upon the future. "The next time we drink this cup together will be in the kingdom of God." The season of Advent is a good time to recover this emphasis of Jesus. Advent is a time of preparation for the arrival of "God with us." So we come to this table not only in remembrance of him, but also in anticipation of him, in anticipation of that time when God's reign will be fulfilled among us.

Jesus said to John and to us, "I am the Alpha and the Omega, the beginning and the end" (Revelation 21:6). The beginning is tied to the end, and the end to the beginning. We will never be closer to heaven in this world than gathered about a manger in an old barn, listening to a young mother gentle her newborn son. Except, possibly, when we gather about his table, remembering and looking forward.

ADVENT II

81 THE GIFT OF SILENCE
Luke 1:5–25

But now, because you did not believe my words, which will be fulfilled
in their time, you will become mute, unable to speak, until the day
these things occur.

Not long ago I heard an Advent sermon, based on Luke 1:5–20, by
Barbara Brown Taylor, one of America's best preachers.[1] I have always
considered the silencing of Zechariah by the angel Gabriel to be a punishment for his unbelief: "...because you did not believe my words,...you
will be mute, unable to speak, until the day these things occur." But,
Taylor suggested, what if the silence was a *gift*, "a wilderness in which
the dream was born"?

Maybe one of the important gifts of Advent is the gift of silence.
There is so much noise during this season; maybe we need to listen for a
while, to be silent before the mystery of God. Taylor recalled a book
review she had seen in which the author was praised for "leaving all the
right things unsaid." Amazing things were happening in those days in
Judah. There was something in the air. And Zechariah received the gift
of "leaving all the right things unsaid," watching in silence as God's
plan unfolded.

Wow! I had never seen this text in that light. It came alive for me in
a new and vital way and has reshaped my approach to Advent this year.
I am a preacher and deeply vested in words. But like a journalist who
appreciates the white space on a page, I appreciate the silent spaces between the words. When I was ordained over twenty years ago, one of
the songs in the service was Simon and Garfunkel's "Sounds of Silence."
I knew even then that somehow I and we had to quieten ourselves and
listen in the silences for the Word of God. The communion we share on
this Advent Sunday seems a wonderful time to leave some things unsaid, to sojourn in the wilderness where dreams are born. No more words
today. Come. Partake. And enjoy, like Zechariah, the gift of silence.

---

[1]Barbara Brown Taylor, a sermon for the annual meeting of the Academy of
Homiletics, preached at Duke University Chapel, Durham, NC, 2 Dec. 1994.

CHRISTMAS I

82 THE MANGER AND THE CROSS
Luke 2:8–14

And suddenly there was with the angel a multitude of the heavenly host praising God and saying, "Glory to God in the highest, and on earth, peace, good will towards men." (KJV)

Communion at Christmas seems a contradiction. Right in the midst of celebrating the birth of Jesus, we pause to commemorate his death. And it is hard to shift gears. We have all heard sermons that speak of the shadow of the cross falling on the manger. There is a large truth there. Birth and death are closely tied. "Unless a grain of wheat fall into the earth and die, it cannot be born again." But it still strikes us as discordant. Consider the powerful closing sentences of Dee Brown's *Bury My Heart at Wounded Knee*. After the massacre of the Sioux at Wounded Knee, South Dakota, in 1890, the few remaining survivors were hauled to the post in wagons.

> The wagonloads of wounded Sioux (four men and forty-seven women and children) reached Pine Ridge after dark. Because all available barracks were filled with soldiers, they were left lying in the open wagons in the bitter cold while an inept army officer searched for shelter. Finally, the Episcopal mission was opened, the benches taken out, and hay scattered over the rough flooring.
>
> It was the fourth day after Christmas in the Year of Our Lord 1890. When the first torn and bleeding bodies were carried into the candlelit church, those who were conscious could see Christmas greenery hanging from the open rafters. Across the chancel front above the pulpit was strung a crudely lettered banner: PEACE ON EARTH, GOOD WILL TO MEN.[2]

It is the very incongruity of it all that touches us. But perhaps it should not. In faith we recognize the contradictions of this world and make our affirmations in the midst of them. What happened at Wounded Knee was wrong. What happened to Jesus on Golgotha was wrong. If we think about that, it makes Christmas a perfect time to celebrate communion. For we not only memorialize a death, we also celebrate a continuing presence. "Christ has died. Christ has risen. Christ shall come again." To share in communion signals our anticipation, our intense expectation of Immanuel, of God with us once again, of things made right at last. There is an old Hebrew custom which says that if a wedding party and a funeral procession meet at an intersection, the funeral

---

[2]Dee Brown, *Bury My Heart at Wounded Knee* (New York: Holt, Rinehart & Winston, 1970), 418.

must give way to the wedding. The past must give way to the future. Death must give way to life. As we come to the table, remember the sacrifices of Jesus Christ, but look forward also to the time when we will meet him face to face and walk together into the Kingdom of God.

CHRISTMAS II

83 THE WORK OF CHRISTMAS
Matthew 25:31–46

"Lord, when was it that we saw you hungry and gave you food, or thirsty and gave you something to drink? And when was it that we saw you a stranger and welcomed you, or naked and gave you clothing? And when was it that we saw you sick or in prison and visited you?" And the king will answer them, "Truly I tell you, just as you did it to one of the least of these who are members of my family, you did it to me."

Of all the wonderful carols we have at Christmastime, none is more dear to me than "Good King Wenceslas." Oh, there are some problems. The name of Christ is not even mentioned and some musicians have called the music trite. But what I like most about it is that it tells a story. And I like stories.

Good King Wenceslas (actually a duke) reigned in Bohemia in the tenth century. During that difficult era Wenceslas was a remarkable man. Of him it was said that he "kept the faith, helping the wretched, feeding the hungry, clothing the naked, protecting widows and orphans, ransoming prisoners, and loving and caring for the rich and poor alike."[3] Alas, as so often happens to such good people, Wenceslas was murdered before his thirtieth birthday, and his saintliness entered into legend.

In the nineteenth century, when hymnist John Mason Neale was searching for a hymnic idea for the Feast of St. Stephen (December 26), the day in England when gifts are given to the poor, his thoughts went to Wenceslas. And the hymn emerged.

In the hymn itself, Wenceslas sees a poor man struggling to gather firewood on a cold winter's eve. He discovers the man's identity and then tells his page:

Bring me flesh and bring me wine,
Bring me pine logs hither.
Thou and I will see him dine
When we bear them thither.

---

[3]Mary Reed Newland, *Good King Wenceslas* (New York: Seabury, 1980), 9.

The eucharistic overtones are striking. We always think of the symbols of Jesus' body and blood as something we receive again and again and again. This sacrifice, we are told, was made for *us*. Perhaps we also need to remember in this season that it was made for others as well. And we have a responsibility to share this gospel with others in word and deed.

Howard Thurman put it this way:

When the song of the angels is stilled,
When the star in the sky is gone,
When the kings and princes are home,
When the shepherds are back with their flock,
The work of Christmas begins:

> To find the lost,
> To heal the broken,
> To feed the hungry,
> To release the prisoner,
> To rebuild the nations,
> To bring peace among brothers and sisters,
> To make music in the heart.[4]

You are invited to share in this feast of thanksgiving as we remember the redeeming love of Good King Jesus and dedicate ourselves to the work of Christmas. And also remember the legacy of Wenceslas:

Ye who will now bless the poor,
Shall yourselves find blessing.

---

[4]Howard Thurman, "The Work of Christmas," in *The Mood of Christmas* (New York: Harper & Row, 1973), 23.

CHRISTMAS III
84 BECRADLED IN COMMUNION
Luke 2:1–7

Christmas is perhaps the most tradition-rich festival we have. The scripture texts, the carols, and the choral music are familiar and beloved. It is therefore difficult for new thoughts and new songs to break into that repertoire. One exception to this, for me, has been Brian Wren's profoundly beautiful "Her Baby, Newly Breathing."[5] I cannot sing this humble carol without being deeply moved, without a huskiness coming into my voice. The simple words invite us into that most intimate of relationships: mother and newborn child.

---

[5]Brian Wren, "Her Baby, Newly Breathing," *Bring Many Names* (Carol Stream, IL: Hope Pub. Co., 1989), 19.

And yet, even in that pacific scene, a jarring note enters. For this child is one "prepared for nail and thorn." How can we hold these thoughts together? What keeps the scene from disintegrating? The grace of God and the genius of the poet. For Wren tells us that the infant strivings of Jesus were "becradled in communion." All of God's power and weakness, all the glory of God-with-us and the pathos of Good Friday, are brought together and cradled with the son of a young woman named Mary.

Those who would look for the essence of the Christian faith, look here. God did not leave us desolate, but chose to share our lives and our fate. The life, death, and resurrection of Jesus are not distinct from the Christmas story. It is all one story. And if we look closely, we can see it all in a rude manger in a cold stable in a nondescript village in a conquered little country: all God's power and glory in a cradle. The communion that there existed between mother and child was as perfect as would be the communion between that child grown-up and God: "not my will but yours." May the communion we share at this table move us closer to that perfection, modeled in cradle and cross, that comes when it is no longer we who live, but Christ who lives in us.

THE NEW YEAR

85 YOU HAVE MADE MY LIFE A BEAUTIFUL SONG   Psalm 47; Revelation 21—22 (selected verses)

Clap your hands, all you peoples; shout to God with loud songs of joy. For the Lord, the Most High, is awesome, a great king over all the earth.

And the one who was seated upon the throne said, "See, I am making all things new."...I John am the one who heard and saw these things. And when I heard and saw them, I fell down to worship at the feet of the angel who showed them to me; but he said to me, "You must not do that! I am a fellow servant with you and your comrades the prophets, and with those who keep the words of this book. Worship God."

Peer Gynt is one of the most tragic figures of world literature. In Ibsen's drama, Peer is one of those people who wants to do good things and is always trying to start over, but never quite does, and ends up wasting his life in reckless and dissolute living. He comes at last, an old man with death at his shoulder, to the hut of the only one who loved him truly and purely. He sees Solveig, old herself and blind, falls on her threshold, and shouts in agony, "Cry out, cry out my sins aloud. Tell me how sinfully I have offended." To which Solveig replies, "You have sinned in nothing, my own dear friend. You have made my life a beautiful song."

Stunned, Peer Gynt says, "Tell me, then—where was my real self, complete and true—the Peer who bore the stamp of God upon his brow?" Solveig answers, "In my faith, in my hope, and in my love." And she takes the old man and rocks him to sleep in her arms.[6]

When I decided for ministry many years ago (or maybe it was the other way around), the day came when I had to tell my father. He listened quietly, with furrowed brow, and then said, "You're going to preach against sin?"

"Yes, sir."

"Well, there should be good job security in that."

And he was right. I have been preaching for almost thirty years now and, to my knowledge, the total quantity of sin in the world has not been significantly lessened. But I am not finished yet, and there are still a lot of sins and sinners that I look forward to having a shot at. People need to be confronted with their sin, made aware of their culpability, and shown a better way. People need to hear the word of God when it says, "I have this against you."[7] But not today. There are times when preachers should not do that. And this is one of them. This is the day for me to say to you what Solveig in her grace and kindness said to Peer Gynt, "You have sinned in nothing, my own dear friends. You have made my life a beautiful song."

Now, does this mean that I do not believe you and I are sinners? Not at all. It means that there are two sides to the human condition, both sin and redemption, and we need to speak to both of them. It means that there are times to cast away stones and times to gather stones together. And I believe that we need a day to be reminded not of the many sins we bear on our spiritual backs, but rather of the stamp of God we bear upon our brow. We need at least one day in which our past—so often a heavy burden, our present—so often boring or depressing, and our future—so often frightening, can be seen lined up in perfect harmony, leading us to God's own glorious future. The year is new and this is a good day for that. And our guides are the ancient Hebrews.

When the new year came to Israel, it was marked with festive celebration. On New Year's Day, the first rays of the sun, rising over the Mount of Olives, shone in a straight line through the outer eastern gate

---

[6]Adapted from Henrik Ibsen, *Peer Gynt*, tr. R. F. Sharp (Garden City: Doubleday, Doran & Co., 1929), 282-286. This story was pointed out to me by Lloyd Averill, a teacher in Washington.

[7]See my sermon "I Have This Against You," in *Preaching through the Apocalypse: Sermons from Revelation* (St. Louis: Chalice, 1992), 69-74.

of the temple, then on across the temple court and over the great altar inside, between the two pillars on either side and on down the long corridor into the holy of holies, the sacred recess at the western end. These first rays of New Year's Day were called "the radiance of God" and symbolized God's entrance into the sanctuary, renewing God's covenant with the people. Just at this moment, the shofar or ram's horn would be sounded, and the procession would begin, saying for the people that God would continue to hold court with them, that they were still Yahweh's people and Yahweh was still their god.[8]

The crops may have failed this year, but it is still God who led us out of Egypt, and that makes all the difference. Psalm 47 traces to this new year's festival: "Clap your hands and shout to God with songs of joy!" Why? Because God gave us our heritage, the pride of Jacob. Because God sits upon the holy throne, reigning over the nations. Because God shall be exalted forever and ever. And on this day we see it, because now the light is just right, and the past, the present, and the future, at least for today, are ordered in a perfect line.

A pretty impressive event. There is something about new beginnings that captures our imagination. We need those times when the "same old stuff" of life lurches from its course and points us in a new direction. But most of all, we need those times when our past, our present, and our future come together, beautifully lined up, making sense, and full of promise. We need a day when we are full of hope and empty of sin.

So how do we make this day a day like that? In a recent panel of the cartoon "Cathy" we see all the employees in her office returning to work after the holidays. One says, "Prioritize, visualize, actualize." Another says, "I am a beautiful and complete human being, freed from all past baggage and on a new path toward dynamic self-realization." And still another says "I have tapped into the power source of my existence and redefined my channels of personal and professional growth." At which point Cathy's boss turns to her and says, "How many days before the motivational tapes they got for Christmas wear off?"[9] Cathy does not reply, and I have nothing against resolutions and motivational tapes, but the answer is probably "not many."

The Bible's answer to our question is a little different. The biblical faith suggests that God is God of the past, the present and, most especially, the future. Time and again in scripture, from Genesis to Revelation, we are reminded that God is continually doing new things. "I'll make me a world," God says. And later, "Behold, I make all things new." There are two interesting things, though, about this newness. First, we do not know the shape of God's future. The biblical descriptions are

---

[8]I owe this history to Don Lindsay and to J. Morgenstern's article "New Year" in *The Interpreter's Dictionary of the Bible* (Nashville: Abingdon, 1962), 3:544-6.

[9]Cathy Guisewite, "Cathy," in the *Fort Worth Star-Telegram*, 4 Jan. 1991, 5:5.

visionary and often in conflict with what we see when we look out our windows. Isaiah sees God making a new world where the wolf and the lamb shall lie down together. The author of Revelation sees a new heaven and a new earth, sees a new Jerusalem coming down from heaven. We see potential war all over the globe; we see wolves in human clothing devouring the lambs of God; we see debt and homelessness and fear. So what are we to do that we might be reassured that the future is in God's hands, that we might be reassured, in Eugene Boring's words, that "everything is going to be all right"? The answer in the last chapter of the Bible summarizes everything that has gone before. Two words: "Worship God!" (22:9). The key to hope for the future rests not in resolutions, but the worship of God. Years and years ago, I heard Granville Walker say in a sermon, "you lose more than just an hour when you don't come to church." And he was right. We lose our future.

The second interesting thing about the affirmation in Revelation that God is making things new is that some of these new things God is doing do not look new at all. They look, well, old. What is the new promise? God will be with us. We will be God's people and God will be our God. That is not new. Go forth, Abraham and Sarah, and I will be with you. Go forth, Moses and Miriam, and I will be with you. And you shall call the baby Emmanuel, which means God is with us. And that means that the new promise involves the best of the old. And that means to get ourselves right, to get ourselves ready, to get ourselves lined up for God's future, we need to bring the best of our past with us.

I know that Paul said, "forgetting what is past, I press on toward the future," but do not believe it. Paul never forgot anything. He just left some things behind. Paul knew what Peer Gynt did not, that the burden of the past can be absorbed in the faith and hope and love of the church and the good can be born again. Bring then your best and leave the rest.

It is true also in our churches. A new year, an old festival. A new ministry, an old presence. A new direction, an old promise. How shall we line them up so that we might experience the radiance of God in our lives? Worship God. Come to the table. Come to the throne of grace in prayer. Listen for the word of God. And when you come forward to be a part of the new things that God will be doing among us, bring the best of your heritage with you. Here, at the gateway to the future, we all stand as one. Even conservatives eventually change. Even liberals build on the past. So bring your love and dedication to the church. Bring your faith in Jesus Christ, the best and truest lover of every human soul. Bring your hope for a world gentled by peace. Bring your love for God and for all God's creation. Bring the best of who you are and who you want to be and cast all that you bring before the throne, to be the very stuff that God uses to make a new world, to make all things new.

Some of you may have heard that, among other things, I am the interim preacher at University Christian Church in Fort Worth until the middle of March. Last Sunday they had their traditional Boar's Head Festival, which is a really big "do." I was in the sanctuary on Thursday, feeling my way toward last Sunday's message, with the hustle and bustle of Boar's Head preparations all about me. Finally, I went over to a woman who looked to be in charge and asked quietly, "Will there be a pulpit for Sunday?" "Oh, yes," she said, "we just swing it out of the way and swing it back when we need it." I thought later to myself, "That is the solidest-looking pulpit I have ever seen. Rock of Gibraltar. Heaven and earth could not move that pulpit!" And now I learn that it just swings out of the way. That is the final word for today. When the new Jerusalem comes down from heaven and all things are one, when there is no need of sun by day or moon by night, because the radiance of God will be all the lights the city will need—the Book of Revelation tells us that there will be beauty and splendor and a crystal river and the tree of life in that city, but there will be no church. No temples, no spires, no pulpits, no preachers, no squeaky chairs in fellowship hall, no solemn Bible study groups. As David Buttrick puts it, "The church is the only organization I know that cheerfully announces its own demise; we know we haven't got forever. In God's great plan we are headed for a phaseout. For who will need churches when God is near at hand?"[10] And he is right!

For me it has been church more than anything else that has brought past and future together in the present. But when the perfect is come and we see God not through a glass darkly, but face to face, the church will just swing out of the way to let us all gather round the throne. It will not be a time of sadness, but gratitude for that old church which served us more faithfully than we deserved, that kept us all in line and looking in the right direction.

I am grateful to you for the privilege of this swinging pulpit and the chance to stand here among us for awhile. Softly as I leave you, I wish each of you great years. You are not worthless sinners, but God's own beloved people with the stamp of God upon your brow. Worship God. Bring your best. And the radiance of God will shine through your eastern gate and illuminate the sacred recesses of your western wall. Amen.

---

[10]Adapted from David Buttrick, "Poetry of Hope," *Preaching through the Apocalypse: Sermons from Revelation*, 161.

EPIPHANY

86 LIVING IN THE CENTURIES[11]
Matthew 1:1–17; Luke 3:23–38

Jesus was about thirty years old when he began his work. He was the son (as was thought) of Joseph son of Heli,...son of David, son of Jesse, son of Obed, son of Boaz,...son of Noah, son of Lamech, son of Methuselah, son of Enoch,...son of Seth, son of Adam, son of God.

In the beginning Epiphany came to us as an exchange of feasts between the Eastern and Western churches, that allowed us to keep Christmas and Epiphany side by side with some rough readjustments of meaning.[12] Epiphany came to signify not so much the birth of Christ, as it had in the East, but Christ's "manifestation" or "appearance"—to the Magi, to Simeon and Anna at the temple, at his baptism under John, at the wedding feast at Cana. If we sandwich the new year celebration between Christmas and Epiphany, as we have in the West, we have a veritable hodgepodge of feasts, all pointing to one of the central dilemmas of the faith: the continuing, enduring presence of God-with-us, coupled with "Behold, I make all things new." Old and new, tradition and change, all come together in this season.

For the Hebrews, the coming of the new year was more than just an occasion for evaluating the year just ended and making promises and predictions for the year to come. It was a time to re-enact and reaffirm the covenant relationship between God and the people, a covenant that reached back centuries into the past. It was an affirmation of what Martin Marty calls not shallow time, but deep time. We often talk about living "just for today," and there is something to be said for that, but it is only half-good advice. We also, like our religious ancestors, need to learn how to live in the centuries. The Jews were the "people of the long nose," not because of their physiognomy, but because they had a long, deep, view of time. When the sun rose on New Year's Day and the king reascended the throne, the people knew that whatever had been in the past year or would be in the new year, God was with them and all would be well.

For us it is the epiphany or manifestation of Christ which gives that assurance. Matthew and Luke go to great pains to assure us that Jesus Christ did did not just appear out of nowhere, but as the culmination of centuries of preparation. Simeon and Anna had been waiting, waiting—for how many years and through how many new year's festivals at the temple?—for the assurance that God really was still with the people.

---

[11]I am indebted for most of the ideas and much of the language in this meditation to Don Lindsay and Bryan Feille.

[12]See Dix, *The Shape of the Liturgy*, 357.

When they saw Jesus, they knew. "My eyes have seen thy salvation." The covenant of presence endures. Without Christ, we are quite lost, but with Christ—born, manifested, crucified, risen, and coming again—we can live not only for today but in and for the centuries.

Reinhold Neibuhr is reported to have said that anything worth doing cannot be completed in one lifetime. We, too, are people of the long nose. We sow seeds we will never harvest and plant trees whose shade we will never enjoy. The manifestation of Christ among us makes that all right. And we come to the table, not just to remember, but to reaffirm the heritage within which we stand. Therefore, dear brothers and sisters, on those days when everything seems to go wrong, remember that Jesus is here. God is with us still. We are going to be all right.

WINTER

87 A CRY OF ABSENCE
2 Timothy 4:19–22

Do your best to come before winter....The Lord be with your spirit. Grace be with you.

There is a remarkable little book by Martin Marty called *A Cry of Absence: Reflections for the Winter of the Heart*. He begins with this affirmation:

> Winterless climates there may be, but winterless souls are hard to picture. A person can count on winter in January in intemperate northern climates, or in July in their southern counterparts. Near the equator, winter is unfelt. As for the heart, however, where can one escape the chill? When death comes, when absence creates pain—then anyone can anticipate the season of cold. Winter can also blow into surprising regions of the heart where it is least expected. Such frigid assaults can overtake the spirit with the persistence of an ice age, the chronic cutting of an Arctic wind.[13]

In response to this acknowledgment, Marty offers a statement by theologian Karl Rahner. Answering a question, Rahner suggested that in the future there would be two types of spirituality, both important, neither chemically pure. The first is the enthusiastic type, the heated-up spirituality of the charismatic and others. The other "would be made up

---

[13]Martin E. Marty, *A Cry of Absence: Reflections for the Winter of the Heart* (San Francisco: Harper, 1983), 1-2.

of those who, although they are committed Christians who pray and receive the sacraments, nevertheless find themselves at home in a wintry sort of spirituality."[14] The first is illustrated by Clarence Macartney's famous sermon "Come Before Winter." I have often read and marvelled at this classic sermon:

> Come before the haze of Indian summer has faded from the fields! Come before the November wind strips the leaves from the trees and sends them whirling over the fields! Come before the snow lies on the uplands and the meadowbrook is turned to ice! Come before the heart is cold! Come before desire has failed! Come before life is over and your probation ended, and you stand before God to give an account of the use you have made of the opportunities in God's grace…granted to you! Come before winter![15]

Stirs the heart, that. But I have often wondered, "What does one do if it is already winter?" Give up? No. That is why I am so grateful for Rahner's second assertion. For I have known that wintry sort of spirituality and feel blessed to have it affirmed as good. The winterfallowed heart rests and, in Marty's words, readies itself for gifts whenever they come.[16] Some of our spirits may indeed be lying winterfallow right now. If so, rest in the faith that God is a god of all seasons and prepare for the gifts that come even in winter. Here is one of them. God loves you immensely and sent Jesus to us as witness to that love. Here are tokens of that love for you, spread on the white tablecloth of winter. Come, partake, receive strength for the journey.

---

[14]Karl Rahner, in Marty, 12.
[15]Clarence Macartney, "Come Before Winter," reprinted in Fant and Pinson, 9:139-140.
[16]Marty, 152.

LENT

 ## DE PROFUNDIS
Luke 5:1–6

When [Jesus] had finished speaking, he said to Simon, "Put out into the deep water…."

The season of Lent is, to my mind, the most unusual season of all. Advent/Christmas is filled with expectation, warmth, and wonder. But Lent is a paradox. On the one hand it is a quieter, more subdued season. The music is softer, the words are measured, the faces are reflective, the ashes linger. On the other hand, the time between Ash Wednesday and

Easter Morn is the most intense Christian time of all. How are we to understand its meaning?

Richard Wing offers this story about how it came to him. He was visiting relatives in the Bahamas when his uncle took him to a pool of fresh water in the middle of an island. Wing was not impressed by the little pool, no more than twenty-five feet across. He described what happened then:

> "Just get your mask on and get in," my uncle said. "Then float straight across the water." I slid down the side of the pool and got my mask in place and then pushed off in order to look down at Lord-knows-what. Immediately I lost my sense of perspective and orientation and desperately, as I remember, lunged for the side of the pool. This was no backyard pool. Once I got my courage and orientation, I floated across a bottomless fresh water cavern, complete with all kinds of colors and nooks and crannies. I was peering straight down over two hundred feet. No one has ever discovered the source or the bottom of this wonder of the world. I grabbed onto the other side. I looked across this "little" pool of water that would never attract the attention of anyone going by. The wind blew. And that image is the closest to God I know: wind off deep water.[17]

Wing goes on to say that this image of God as wind off deep water reminds him of Lent: a time of wonder, mystery, and reflection. Reading Wing's article stirs my own memory.

I once served a church in New York City that met in an old Gothic sanctuary. I sat at the side of the chancel next to the choir and when the elements of the supper were passed, we took the bread and cup and partook in our own time. High above me there was a light recessed in the vault of the ceiling that shone down on where I sat. And when I would sit with that little cup in my hands, a tiny pinpoint of light, coming from far above me, would dance and play, dive and swim, in the royal purple of that cup. That tiny point of light became very important to me. The cup itself was dark and deep and rich and somber, not unlike the blood of the Savior it represented. But the point of light was not afraid of it. It ran and somersaulted across the cup as if to say to the blood, "You can't catch me; you can't kill me. I'm alive!"

Wind. And light. And how many more images are there for the heights and depths of our faith. Lent is a time to reflect on these high and deep matters. What Jesus said to Peter, he also says to us, "Put out into the deep water...." And I know of no better setting for reflection that profound than sitting quietly in church, holding a communion cup in your hand.

---

[17]Richard A. Wing, "Soundings," University Christian Church *Reporter* XV:13, San Diego, California, 27 March 1990.

PALM SUNDAY

 ALL THE DONKEYS OF THE BIBLE[18]
John 12:12–16

Do not be afraid, daughter of Zion. Look, your king is coming, sitting on a donkey's colt.

According to Jill Pelaez, there is a funny little place outside Madrid in Spain that is called Pablo's Donkey Farm.[19] It was not always a donkey farm. Once it was just a farm. But Pablo had a way with donkeys. He could heal them when they were sick and change their attitudes when they were obnoxious. Pretty soon everyone in the region came to Pablo's to buy, sell, trade, and have their donkeys healed. To the exasperation of his wife, Pablo's own farming suffered. One man who brought a sick donkey said, "Surely donkeys are your business," but Pablo's wife answered, "No, Pablo is a farmer, but for love of donkeys, he does not farm."[20] Finally Pablo realized the nature of his calling, surrendered to it, and changed the name of his operation to Pablo's Donkey Farm.

Sounds like a place where they might send old preachers to bray away their declining years in the pasture! But there is a jewel in this story, and it is the love of donkeys. People have almost always loved donkeys and donkey stories, especially young people. At the petting zoo, the donkey is the most popular animal, and everyone wants a ride. In literature it is the same. The adventures of the young man turned into a donkey in Apuleius' *The Golden Ass* have delighted readers for almost two thousand years and influenced many other tales, like that from Shakespeare's *A Midsummer Night's Dream* and even *Pinocchio*. John Westerhoff tells a Sufi story about a smuggler named Nasrad'im, who led his pack donkeys across the border every day. The border guards knew he was smuggling something and they searched his donkeys stem to stern, but never found a thing. Finally he retired, a wealthy man, at age thirty and threw a party for the border guards. The guards said, "Nasrad'im, we know you were smuggling, but we couldn't catch you. Now that it's over, please—tell us what you were smuggling?" He answered, "Donkeys."[21] And no one can read of the love between Yannakos and his donkey Youssoufaki in *The Greek Passion* by Kazantzakis without being deeply touched. I once lived in Africa for two years, and I used to watch the young people play and race with their donkeys like young Americans do with cars. More fun, I thought. And safer. Oh, how

---

[18]The sermon from which this meditation is excerpted was first preached on the National Radio Pulpit in 1982.

[19]See Jill Pelaez, *Donkey Tales* (Nashville: Abingdon, 1971), 9-19.

[20]*Ibid.,* 15-16.

[21]John Westerhoff, "The Pilgrimage" in *The Pilgrimage of Christian Faith* (Atlanta: Catacomb Cassettes, 1980).

we love to watch the children on Palm Sunday as they climb into the chancel in their choir robes to sing joyfully their praise of that little gray donkey, the little gray donkey that gave Jesus a ride.

The love of donkeys *is* a lovely image, and it is a biblical image, too. The Bible is full of donkey stories; it occurred to me that I might build a happy, uplifting Palm Sunday message for you by looking at some of them. So I set out to try to find every donkey passage in the Bible...and when I did, you will not believe what happened. As I read...slowly, seductively, a very strange pattern began to emerge. Let me tell you about it:

- Genesis 22: Abraham rose early in the morning, saddled his donkey, and took two of his young men and Isaac with him. An innocent ram appeared in the thicket, and he was killed in Isaac's place.

- Numbers 22: Balaam rose in the morning, saddled his donkey, and went with the princes of Moab...and later the tribe of Israel slew Balaam with the sword.

- 1 Samuel 25: Abigail mounted her donkey and rode to King David, where she betrayed her husband, Nabal. She returned to Nabal, and when he heard the news, he died.

- 2 Samuel 17: When Ahithopel, David's counselor, saw that his advice was not followed, he saddled his donkey and went home. He set his house in order, hanged himself, and died.

- 1 Kings 2: Shemei rose and saddled his donkey and went to seek his slaves....Solomon was angry, and he sent Benaiah to find Shemei; Benaiah went out, found Shemei, struck him down, and he died.

- 1 Kings 13: A donkey was saddled for the old prophet from Judah. As he rode away a lion met him on the road and killed him, and the lion and the donkey stood beside his body.

What in the world is going on? Enough of this! I could go on, but that is enough. I did not expect to find this. The donkey is a peaceable animal, not given to violence. And yet, almost every time in the Bible that someone gets on a donkey to ride, something or somebody dies! There is no explanation for this in any of the commentaries I have looked at or in other books I have seen. It is uncanny and mysterious, but like Coleridge's albatross, the donkey is a strange harbinger of death in the Bible. Toward the end of my survey, every time I found a scripture about a donkey I flinched, wondering who was going to die next. Let me give you just one more:

> Fear not, daughter of Zion. Behold, your king is coming, sitting on a donkey....And they took [him] to the place of the skull, which is called in Hebrew Golgotha. There they crucified him...(John 12:15, 19:17-18 RSV).

Well, well. I have learned two things from this little study of mine. The first is that it will be a cold day in Hades before I get on a donkey again. And the second thing I have learned for a certainty is that Jesus *knew*! He really knew, but he sent his disciples to fetch the donkey and he rode into town anyway. It is just *too* clear: from his prophecies about the suffering of the Son of Man, from his understanding of the universal law that says he who would save others cannot save himself, right down to the four-footed transportation he chose for his ride to destiny, Jesus knew that he was going to town for the last time; he knew that he would never see Galilee again.

Suddenly we realize that there is death in the good news and the loving images that we preach. William Stringfellow once wrote that apart from God, death is the strongest force in the world,[22] and here we see it, so woven into the gospel that we cannot get it out. G. K. Chesterton points out the paradox in this animal that we burden with so much life and death. "With monstrous head and sickening cry and ears like errant wings," is the donkey. But, in Chesterton's words:

> Starve, scourge, deride me: I am dumb;
> I keep my secret still.
> Fools! For I also had my hour;
> One far, fierce hour and sweet.
> There was a shout about my ears,
> And palms before my feet![23]

Yes! The donkey—harbinger of death, starved and scourged—had and has its hour and its task: to carry us to and through Jerusalem to new life on the other side. The genius and the grace and the joy of the Christian faith is that, with Jesus, death becomes not the end, but part of the pilgrimage toward a new beginning. Just a few lines after the scripture we have been looking at in the Gospel of John, Jesus says, "unless a grain of wheat falls into the earth and dies, it remains alone, but if it dies it bears much fruit." St. Francis put it another way when he said, "It is by dying that we are born to eternal life." So at the heart of the good news is a gospel of death *and* resurrection. Jesus got on the donkey and rode to Jerusalem, and he knew what that meant. We have got a ticket to ride, too. And only if we are willing to let our old selves die is there hope for renewal, rebirth, resurrection. Our gathering about this table today is a witness to that truth. We look not only back, but also forward, to the journey we will make to new life in Christ.

On one of the most spectacular days of my life I sailed on a Greek ship to the island of Santorini. We came through a group of small is-

---

[22]William Stringfellow, *An Ethic for Christian and Other Aliens in a Strange Land* (Waco: Word, 1973), 68.

[23]Excerpted from G. K. Chesterton, "The Donkey," *A Chesterton Anthology* (San Francisco: Ignatius Press, 1985), 1.

lands and then straight toward the solid wall of a cliff that loomed larger and larger as we approached. And then, there we were, standing at the bottom of that incredible wall, so high that we could barely see the top. We knew that the city was up there somewhere, but how were we ever to get up? Just then some boys came up with some rather disheveled-looking donkeys, and we got on and started up the switchback trail. The donkey I was riding was very purposeful and, thank God, surefooted. He knew that his task in life was to get me to the mountaintop. And he did his job very well. From the top I could see the whole panorama of the joyous village, the island, and the sea. I had been in the midst of a serious illness and depression when I arrived on Santorini. But I experienced a resurrection of the spirit on that day, and it was a donkey that took me up the mountain.

Jesus saw the donkey come for him, and he knew, and he was not afraid. Abraham Lincoln, Martin Luther King, Jr., John Kennedy, and so many others have fought for life in our world. And when the donkey came for them, like all the donkeys in the Bible had done, they did not shrink from the moment, but said, "Come, my good friend. Could you give me a lift up the mountain?" Somewhere on the way, they fell asleep; but they woke up at the top in the city of God.

Fear not, daughter of Zion. Behold, your king is coming, sitting on a donkey's colt. The gospel is for the people. It is a gospel of power, greater power than the world has ever known. And the gospel, like the donkey, will carry us to the mountain top. Like the donkey, it will carry us home. For the love of donkeys does not mean the love of death, but rather the love of God which triumphs over it.

Although we may doubt it during this difficult week, early next Sunday morning the triumph of that love will be proved once again. And we shall have hope. Listen to this tender story from *The Greek Passion*. A poor man named Yannakos comes to his faithful donkey after Easter and says:

> "Ah, Youssoufaki, the holiday's over. Christ is risen! We've had a good time; you can't complain. I've brought you double rations…and cut fresh grass for you. You're such a beauty! What would become of me without you…?

> "And today I'm bringing you a piece of news that'll please you. Next Easter the Passion of Christ will be acted in the village [once again]; you must have heard talk of it. They need a donkey. Well, I asked the notables, as a favor, that you, Youssoufaki, should be that donkey of the holy Passion. It's on your back that Christ will enter Jerusalem. What an honor for you.…You'll march at the head, carrying Christ; they'll make you a carpet of myrtles and palms, and the grace of God will descend upon your back [and] all your hide will shine like silk.

"And when I die, if God is willing to let me, poor sinner that I am, into Paradise, I shall stop at the gate, I shall kiss the porter's hand and I shall say to him: 'I've a favor to ask you, Apostle Peter; it's that he may enter Paradise, that we may go in together: otherwise, I'm not going in!' And the Apostle will burst out laughing, and stroke your rump, and say: 'All right, I'll do that for you, Yannakos; get on Youssoufaki and ride in; God loves donkeys.'

"'And then what joy, my Youssoufaki! Eternal joy! You will walk about with none of these heavy baskets, no load, no pack saddle, in fields where there'll be immortal clover, this high, coming right up to your mouth so you won't have the bother of stooping. In Heaven you'll bray every morning to wake the angels. They'll laugh. As light as down, they'll get on your back, and you'll walk through the meadows together....'"[24]

Dear friends, it is hard for us to see from here to those meadows of heaven where angels, children, and donkeys play. Sometimes it gets very dark here, and we cannot even see past Friday. But we need to remember that the night is often darkest just before the dawn. And however we may fear that ride into the unknown, if we will look carefully in the first gray light of dawn, we may see a sight that will convince us once and for all that death shall have no dominion, that resurrection and renewal are at hand, that Jesus shall reign. For if we strain our eyes, we can see a man walking down a lonely road, leading a donkey. On the donkey sits a woman who is great with child, riding toward her destiny... and ours. The donkey is walking slowly, steadily, patiently, purposefully, and eternally toward Bethlehem.

May this Holy Week be that for you, and make all the weeks of your lives holy ones. Do not stop searching for the new life that is to come. For the love of donkeys. For the love of Christ.

---

[24]Kazantzakis, *The Greek Passion*, tr. Jonathan Griffin (New York: Simon and Schuster, 1954), 49-50.

MAUNDY THURSDAY

90 PERHAPS WE SHALL NOT BREAK BREAD AGAIN   Matthew 26:26–29

While they were eating, Jesus took a loaf of bread, and after blessing it he broke it, gave it to the disciples, and said, "Take, eat, this is my body." Then he took a cup, and after giving thanks he gave it to them, saying, "Drink from it, all of you; for this is my blood of the covenant, which is poured out for many for the forgiveness of sins. I tell you, I will never again drink of this fruit of the vine until that day when I drink it new with you in my Father's kingdom.

Early in the Passover Seder, the question is asked, "Why is this night not like other nights?" and the response focuses upon the special way in which the people had been blessed by God on this night of nights. The special blessing that we celebrate makes *this* a night unlike other nights as well, for on this Thursday evening in a small room the Lord's Supper that we hold so dear was instituted. Jesus and his disciples were gathered for the last supper they would share in this world. The disciples would never forget it. And neither can we.

There is something special about first times: the first time you catch a fish, kiss a girl or boy, drive a car. There is also something special about last times: the last time you play for the school team, sleep in your old room, see your parents. At the close of my two years in the Peace Corps in Africa, I gathered with all my brother and sister volunteers for termination conference. The last night we had a dinner together. It was a very touching evening; there were lots of tears and hugs, and there were promises to keep in touch…but I think we knew better. We knew that it was the end of our time together, and that we would probably never see each other again. It was our last supper. And I have not, in these past twenty-five years, seen one of those dear people. From time to time the faces and the memories come to me, give me pause, and make me smile. And, lest I forget, I keep an African woodcarving on the wall of my room wherever we move to remind me of those days and those friends. Perhaps you have similar times and people in your past that are precious to you and ways of reminding yourself about them.

Holy communion is one of those most special of times. The other day I was reading Kahlil Gibran's interpretation of the Last Supper according to Matthew and, while I do not want for a minute to elevate Gibran to the status of scripture, I believe his interpretation sheds some interesting light on the supper.

Here is a paragraph from his book *Jesus, the Son of Man*:

Then Jesus took a loaf of bread and gave it to us, saying, "Perhaps we shall not break bread again. Let us eat this morsel in remembrance of our days in Galilee." And he poured wine from a jug into a cup and he drank, and gave to us, and he said, "Drink this in remembrance of a thirst we have known together. And drink it also in hope for the new vintage. When I am enfolded and am no more among you, and when you meet here or elsewhere, break the bread and pour the wine, and eat and drink even as you are doing now. Then look about you; and perchance you may see me sitting with you at the board."[25]

Four things catch my attention. The first is Jesus saying to his disciples, "Perhaps we shall not break bread again. Let's eat this morsel in remembrance of our days in Galilee." This is pathos at its highest, a touching sadness, and so very human. Things had gone bad for Jesus and his disciples; there was death in the air, and they knew it. How different from those early heady days in Galilee when they had the world on a string. The crowds were flocking to them, and they had visions of saving the world. And there was joy and laughter; those were the days. Jesus says, "Let's remember those days," and the others nod and smile. It is a scene reminiscent of the Whiffenpoofs as we see this small group in the upper room with their glasses raised on high, toasting *auld lang syne*, knowing that it is the last time they will be together.

But there is more to this than just remembering the good times. Jesus says, "Let's drink in remembrance of a thirst we have known together." For they had not only been happy together, they had suffered together, especially lately. They had known privation and would know more, but they had also shared their thirsty spirits. They had thirsted for God and sought for God together. Sociologists know that the deepest bonds are forged in people when they have a common cause or mission or purpose. The best image of a successful relationship is not clenched hands, where two people are totally wrapped up in one another, but the ancient image of praying hands, where the people are not wrapped up together, but side by side and pointed in the same direction. And this small group of people had been pointed in the same direction. Jesus and the disciples had looked for God together. That is thirsty work. So now, Jesus and his friends lift a glass to that. And I wonder if, as they did, they saw beyond the cross and the tomb to a rising church that would remember and endure and share the thirst.

Then Jesus says something else. Do not just eat and drink in remembrance of the good times and the hard times. Eat and drink "in hope for the new vintage." While I was in New York, I lived one summer in the basement of Robert Crichton's house. He was the author of that wonderful book, *The Secret of Santa Vittoria*. He once described how joyous and tense it was, how filled with expectation and dread, when a new vintage was being prepared in a small Italian village. The scene made

---

[25]Kahlil Gibran, *Jesus the Son of Man* (New York: Alfred A. Knopf, 1959), 195.

its way into the book.[26] You may recall: the grapes have been harvested, stomped, made into wine…and then came the moment of truth. Would the vintage be good or average or poor…or perhaps even spectacular? The people lived on hope. And Jesus is telling his disciples that they are to do the same. Live in the hope of a new vintage, a new bubbling up of the Spirit of God within people that will transform the shape of things to come.

Eat and drink, Jesus says, to remember and to hope. That atmosphere makes for a special meal, and indeed it was. But if that were all that was involved, we would not be gathered about this table today. It was the last thing said by Jesus that was crucial. "When I am no more among you and when you meet here or elsewhere, break the bread and pour the wine and eat and drink even as you are doing now. Then look around you, and perchance you may see me sitting with you at the board." If you will gather around this table and eat and drink in memory and in hope, perchance you will see me. And that is the key.

Not just to remember. Not just to hope. But to re-envision the living Christ as a vital part of our ongoing lives as persons and as a church. For the Lord's Supper, more than memory and hope, is a time of meeting and making known. Carlyle Marney once wrote that a friend told him that the archaeologist Romanoff uncovered what, to him, was incontrovertible evidence that behind the rubbish next to a Jerusalem wall, he had discovered the grave of Jesus. However, he had been persuaded not to publish the evidence because of the harm it might do. Marney said,

> Rubbish! Let him publish! Let him publish all he knows! It couldn't hurt. Because this is not where he said he would meet us. Not by a rubbish heap. Not behind any wall. Find the old wood of the cross; find all kind of graves. He said he would meet us at neither cross nor grave; he said he would meet us at his table.[27]

Marney is right. Perchance you may see me sitting with you. It is the re-enactment of this ancient feast that allows us not just to see but also to recognize Jesus Christ, and know that he continues in our midst. It was on the road to Emmaus, you remember, where two of Jesus' disciples met a stranger and invited him home, this after Jesus had already been crucified and buried. They sat down at table and the stranger broke the bread; and the text says that their eyes were opened, and he was made known to them in the breaking of the bread (Luke 24:13-35). It is when we come to this table as we should that we sometimes catch a glimpse of him: in the face of a friend, in a note of the organ, in the thought of a moment, in a feeling that comes, in a twinge of the con-

---

[26]Robert Crichton, *The Secret of Santa Vittoria* (New York: Simon and Schuster, 1966), 405-416.

[27]Carlyle Marney, *The Crucible of Redemption* (Nashville: Abingdon, 1968), 48.

science, in a leap of the heart, in a stillness of the soul, in a way that we cannot always explain, Christ makes himself known to us.

People around the world, no matter their creed or confession, are coming to the table tonight to celebrate Holy Thursday. They will come for many reasons. They will come for remembrance; they will come out of hope; they will come because they might meet Christ here and find him made known to them. What joy it is to join them! If this is your first time to partake of communion, you are very welcome. Not one of us knows if this might also be the last time we are permitted to come to the table. It is so good to be here.

Jesus took the loaf and said, "Perhaps we shall not eat this bread again, so let's taste a morsel together and remember the good days." And he took a cup and said, "Friends, we have shared the same thirst, we've been pointed in the same direction together, let's drink to that sharing and that thirstiness that only God can quench and as we do, let's hope for the new vintage, the new life in the spirit that may come to all of us."

Finally he said, "I must go now, but whenever you do this, look around you and perchance you may see me at the table with you." Let it be so. O God, we thank you for the memories, for the thirst, for the hope, and for the presence, as we come to this table together in the spirit and in the name of Christ.

GOOD FRIDAY

91 THE WORST AND BEST
Mark 15:21–47

Then Jesus gave a loud cry and breathed his last....it was...the day before the sabbath.

In his book *The Youngest Day,* Robert Farrar Capon says this:

Every Sunday when Christians meet, they break bread and drink wine because they were commanded to "do this in remembrance of me." Specifically, they gather in special and sometimes opulent buildings—frequently having dressed themselves to the nines—and they proceed, to the accompaniment of expensively produced music and fairly ambitious choreography, to sing and trip their way lightly through the fantastic business of recalling how, on a hill far away, they once kicked the living bejesus out of God incarnate in Christ. They take the worst thing the human race has ever done and make it the occasion of a celebration. And why? *Because the worst things humans did was also the best thing God did.* The Friday was Good.

What that suggests to me is that when God remembers evil, God re-members it as we remember the crucifixion in Communion: in the light of the good God has brought out of it.[28]

William K. McElvaney has suggested that there is a saving possi-bility in every situation. That is easy enough to accept for many of the irksome little situations that we find ourselves in. But to say that of the crucifixion is large: the worst thing we ever did becomes the best thing God ever did. Monstrous evil becomes the gateway for the salvation of the world. As McElvaney says:

The saving possibility which is given in every situation may not be the one you wanted, the one you would have chosen, the one you were looking for; you may not perceive it, but its presence does not depend on whether you see it or not, because the saving possibility is there.[29]

Consider the cross. Look at what we did. Then look at what God did. We bow in wonder at such power, such wisdom, and such love. And we come to the table in penitence and thanksgiving.

---

[28]Robert Farrar Capon, *The Youngest Day* (San Francisco: Harper, 1983), 89. Capon's story was pointed out to me by Richard A. Wing.
    [29]William K. McElvaney, *The Saving Possibility* (Nashville, Abingdon, 1971), 67.

EASTER

92   WHO'S RISEN FROM JOSEPH'S TOMB?[30]
1 Corinthians 15:12–19, 51–58

… if Christ has not been raised, then our proclamation has been in vain and your faith has been in vain.

We have gathered to watch the "Son" come up. We have come to celebrate the resurrection of Christ. We have come at the break of day to break bread and, in doing so, receive the inbreaking of God's world-renewing Spirit. It is a new day and a new world. "Lo, I tell you a mys-tery." Paul was certainly right about that. I tell you a mystery: the per-ishable must put on the imperishable and the mortal must put on immor-tality. Today is the day which makes that mysterious affirmation cred-ible, instead of pure nonsense. Because in this, the great resurrection chapter of 1 Corinthians, Paul admits that if Christ has not been raised, then all of this is nonsense and we are of all people to be most pitied. So the resurrection of Christ is the most important affirmation that Chris-tians have to make. How easy or how difficult is that affirmation for

---

[30]Adapted from a sermon originally preached at Texas Christian University's Easter sunrise service, April 3, 1988.

you? And when you say "Christ is risen," what do you mean?

When I answered the telephone, a rhythmic voice said to me: "Mr. Jet-er, if you can answer one simple question, then you will be eligible for our grand prize giveaway. And here's that question: 'Who's buried in Grant's Tomb?'" Silence. More silence. "Uhh, Mr. Jet-er, is the question too difficult?"

I finally answered that, well, it was a very complex and difficult question; that—off the top of my head—I could think of at least four or five answers I could make a case for:

- There is the obvious answer: Grant. But like a lot of obvious answers, it is only partially true.
- Then there is the historical answer. As one who lived across the street from Grant's Tomb in New York City for five years, I can assure you that the mortal remains of Ulysses S. **and** Julia D. Grant are there. (And, by the way, they are sepulchered, not buried.)
- Moving right along, there is a theological sense in which the answer to the question "Who's buried in Grant's tomb?" is, of course, "No one." There are two old corpses there, but no one is at home in them.
- And, finally, a philosophical answer, if you will. Nobody usually mispronounces my name "Jet-er" except people who do not know me but call me on the phone wanting to sell me something; so my answer is colored by my wondering just what, in the long run, my answer is going to cost me.

"So you see, it is not an easy question at all."

Silence. More silence. Click.

Is that not just like a professor? You ask him or her what time it is and she or he tells you how to make a watch. And is that not one of the problems with coming to college? Many things that were once clear grow murky. The reason we call that education is because they *are* murky and will only become truly clear when you have passed them through the crucible of your own struggle and pain and growth.

I was at a birthday party for the daughter of a friend of ours. At one point she took me aside and announced to me with great seriousness, "Joey, I'm four now. I know everything." I simply nodded, because at four, you have it covered. You can communicate and get around and do things and you have not been to school yet to mess everything up. Even at my age I would prefer sometimes not to have to "go to school" on the matter of resurrection.

Because if the phone rings now and I discover that I can qualify for the grand prize giveaway by answering the question, "Who's buried— or better, risen—from Joseph of Arimathea's tomb?" I know deep down that that question is so large that it goes cleaving through the infinite.

At a time like this, five-thirty in the morning on the first day of the week, the obvious answer to the question of the resurrection is probably the best one, probably my four favorite words in the whole New Testament: "He is not here" (Mark 16:7). We come to this charnel house, to this place of death, and Christ simply is not here. Death could not hold the beloved child of God. "Alleluia, Christ is risen." And yet, to say that Christ is risen is to say more, much more than that a dead man has been resuscitated. Historically, we see its effect on people, on the world. As Leslie Weatherhead told it, if we had gone to the upper room in Jerusalem on Good Friday night, we would have found the door shut and barred. Inside would have been a small group of despairing, humiliated, trembling men and women.

> Life was over for them....They had hoped that Jesus was the Messiah who would redeem Israel. He had promised so much and they had believed him. But now he was dead and they were stuck here, frightened...and in danger. But suppose you had gone back to the same house a week later. The windows would have been open, the doors unbarred. Through them we might have heard laughter and the singing of psalms and the plans of those who, within a few weeks of the murder of Christ, were preaching his gospel and declaring his risen glory.[31]

After Easter, Mary was changed from a mourner to a messenger, Thomas was changed from a doubter to a believer, Peter was changed from a denier to a preacher, Paul later on was changed from a persecutor to a missionary, and that small band in the upper room was changed from a sniveling band of has-beens to the Church of Jesus Christ! And we know that for a historical fact.

But wait, there is still more. When David Buttrick was on our campus last month he reminded us that those first Christians did not understand the resurrection historically, but apocalyptically. God has broken into history in the most compelling way imaginable. Jesus had come preaching God's new order. His death had re-established the order of the first century. And now the resurrection has reversed that old dying order. The new order of God has begun and the risen Christ is its head. To say that Christ is risen is to say that the mission of the church is credible; it is to say that we no longer live and die as pagans without hope; it is to say that all things, all things are made new.[32]

Finally, my response to the question of Easter is colored by my wondering just what, in the long run, my answer is going to cost me. I know for a certainty that, as long as Jesus stays dead, I can go ahead and take care of business, because nothing matters overmuch, and the paths of glory lead but to the grave. But, if Christ is risen, then who we are, what we do, and what we become matter immensely, because we are a part of God's great affirmation of life flung against the darkness of a dying

---

[31]Leslie Weatherhead, "The Sunday after Easter," in Fant and Pinson, 11:120.
[32]See David Buttrick, *Preaching Jesus Christ* (Philadelphia: Fortress, 1988), 57-68.

universe. And my being a part of that process may cost me everything I have.

Richard Lischer has pointed out that the resurrection accounts are always followed by a "therefore," always connected with the stories of our lives.[33] The biblical writers knew this. Christ is risen, *therefore* (Romans 5) we have peace with God. Christ is risen, *therefore* (Romans 8) there is no condemnation for those who are in Christ. Christ is risen, *therefore* (Acts 3) repent of your sins and turn again that times of refreshing may come. Christ is risen, *therefore* (1 Corinthians 15, our text for the day) be steadfast, immovable, always abounding in the work of God.

There we have it then: obvious, historical, theological answers, never forgetting the question of cost. Where do you find yourself in that spectrum today? Or do you find yourself in another place altogether? As the glorious light of Easter morn is refracted through the lenses of our experience, we see many different things. Some of us tend toward the purple and blue and green. Others tend toward the yellow and orange and red. But I hear Paul telling us that is all right, because resurrection is a many-splendored thing. "Listen, I will tell you a mystery," he says. And the point is not for us to approach Easter in some kind of reductionistic way about rekindling amino acids or reknitting cellular molecules or whatever; the point is for us to embrace the mystery—the mystery that begins with the simple affirmation that "he is not here," and runs all the way to the greatest affirmation of all, "I am making all things new."

The mystery of the resurrection is the mystery of life itself. I do not understand why the grass in my lawn that is fertilized, watered, and nurtured refuses to grow, while other grass has grown up through my driveway, defying herbicides, bursting and buckling its way through four solid inches of concrete. But in my frustration I find room to smile at that. Nor do I understand how the sun comes up or how a bit of bread and a sip of wine remind me so powerfully of Jesus. God's ways are not our ways. But I do understand why. I do understand that God loves life and will not let death have the last word. Wherever we find ourselves, we can all give thanks for the many splendors of Easter, for the mysterious love of God that passes all understanding and makes all things new.

Harvey Cox tells of one Easter celebration that was scheduled for 4:00 a.m. at a Boston discotheque. There was liturgy and food and music and dance. He describes the end of the service this way:

> After the benediction we greeted one another with the Kiss of Peace. Again the discotheque swayed and sang. A Resurrection light collage leaped onto the walls. Since the hall is equipped with twenty-six pro-

---

[33]Richard Lischer, "'Resurrexit': Something to Preach," *The Christian Century* 97:12 (2 April 1980), 371-73.

jectors, the effect was like moving in an instant from a dim cave into a cathedral of luminous windows. Just as the collage was reaching its apex with the Beatles singing "Here Comes the Sun," someone threw open the back door. By some miracle of celestial timing, the sun was just beginning to peek over the Boston extension of the Massachusetts Turnpike.[34]

And now as our service draws to a close, that miracle is repeated as the sun begins to peek over the library. The "Son" is up. And **Christ** is risen from Joseph's tomb. Thanks be to God forever and ever.

---

[34]Harvey Cox, *The Seduction of the Spirit* (New York: Simon and Schuster, 1973), 158.

SPRING

93 BENEATH THE FACE OF DEATH
Luke 9:51–56

When the days drew near for him to be taken up, he set his face to go to Jerusalem.

In Luke 9:51 we read that "When the days drew near for him to be taken up, he set his face to go to Jerusalem." The words speak of determination, of no turning back. And it sounds as if the good days of his ministry are over, that nothing else remains except suffering, rejection, and death. At least that is what I thought.

Then I happened to read *Their Eyes Were Watching God*, a magnificent novel by Zora Neale Hurston, which tells the story of the emergence of a black woman in the old South. Janie is abused by her husband, who finally dies. Hurston describes the funeral like this:

> Janie starched and ironed her face and came set in the funeral behind the veil. It was like a wall of stone and steel. The funeral was going on outside. All things concerning death and burial were said and done. Finish. End. Nevermore. Darkness. Deep hole. Dissolution. Eternity. Weeping and wailing outside. Inside the expensive black folds were resurrection and life. She did not reach outside for anything, nor did the things of death reach inside to disturb her calm. She sent her face to Joe's funeral, and herself went rollicking with the springtime across the world.[35]

---

[35]Zora Neale Hurston, *Their Eyes Were Watching God* (Urbana: Univ. of Illinois Press, 1978), 136-137. Originally published in 1937.

Amazing! As I read of Janie, I immediately thought of Jesus. When he "starched and ironed his face" to go to Jerusalem, what was going on behind his face? Was he frightened and nervous or content and calm? I choose to believe the conviction that he was on track, following God's will, and doing an eternally good thing consoled him in his journey toward the cross. I choose to believe that with the scent of death growing all around him, he could look from behind his set face and see the springtime of God's new age just beyond. And, finally, I choose to believe that as we surround this table to memorialize his death, we too can see resurrection, new life, and Jesus there bidding us to come and go rollicking with him through the new world that God is bringing into being. Broken body. Bread. Spilled blood. Wine. All of this in front of us. And they are very real. But they are not all there is. For the mind's eye of hope sees beyond the numbness of loss to the springtime of our salvation.

Thanks be to God.

MOTHER'S DAY

94 CRUMBY FAITH AND TELLING THE TRUTH
Mark 7:24–30

He said to her, "Let the children be fed first, for it is not fair to take the children's food and throw it to the dogs." But she answered him, "Sir, even the dogs under the table eat the children's crumbs." Then he said to her, "For saying that, you may go—the demon has left your daughter." So she went home, found the child lying on the bed, and the demon gone.

Almost every week we hear of those persons, women and men alike, who give of themselves that otherwise unwanted children can know love and attention and home. Early this past week I read of a woman, an orphan herself, who is now in the process of raising twenty-three children. On Friday there was a news item about a woman who has become known as "Grandma Baby." The number of children she has raised now approaches one hundred. These people preach Mother's Day sermons with their lives much better than I can with words. All I can do is reflect on the mystery and the wonder, the joy and agony of parenting. And I intend to do that.

When I found out I was to preach before you on Mother's Day, I decided to take this task seriously, to try to wade through the syrup that generally characterizes Mother's Day sermons to arrive at the higher ground of biblical faith. And so I chose the text you have heard, surely one of the more puzzling texts in the Bible.

Used by the church to make the case for the inclusion of Gentiles in the faith community, it has, like an onion, other layers.[36] There are so many questions. What was Jesus doing in Tyre and Sidon anyway? This was not his turf. How did the woman hear about him, and who was she anyway? Mark describes her politically, a Syrophoenician woman, while Matthew describes her religiously, a Canaanite woman. And the most puzzling thing of all: Why did Jesus speak to her so cruelly? Commentators have tried to soften the passage by saying that this was simply a rhetorical device of Jesus to put the woman to the test.[37] But that hardly washes, does it? There seems to be no escaping the fact that Jesus, at this point anyway, still identifies his mission as one to the lost sheep of Israel and not to the Gentile world.

But no matter. The fascinating thing about this text is not its implications for a multinational gospel, but rather the human interaction between Jesus and the mother of a child. In some way, we know not how, this woman, whose daughter was seriously ill, found out that Jesus was present, went to him, and begged him to heal her little girl. Jesus said, "It is not right to take the children's bread and throw it to the dogs." Ouch! Had it been I, I suspect I would have told Jesus what he could do with his precious Jewish bread and stormed out.

But she did not. She said, "Sir, even the dogs under the table eat the children's crumbs." And you can almost see Jesus sitting there with his mouth open. All through the Gospels Jesus outwits one person after another. But not here. Martin Luther, never at a loss for words, whopped his belly and said of Jesus, "He is silent as a stick. Look, this is really a hard thump. Her reply was a masterpiece."[38] And it was. When Jesus finally spoke, I suspect that it was with a smile that he said, "You may go your way; the demon has left your daughter."

Somehow this story reminds me of my grandmother. She was no systematic theologian, no metaphysician, no scholar. She never gathered the whole loaf of faith together in one grand system. Rather, hers was a crumby faith. When the biblical message, the exigencies of this world and her personal experience collided—as they will do—she picked up the crumbs from those encounters and stored them away. The whole loaf of faith was never given to her, so she built her own loaf, one crumb at a time, until she put it all together.

---

[36]See Sharon H. Ringe, "A Gentile Mother's Story," in *Feminist Interpretation of the Bible*, ed. Letty M. Russell (Philadelphia: Westminster, 1985), 65-72. See also Paul E. Scherer, "A Gauntlet with a Gift in It," in *Interpretation* 20:4 (October 1966), 387-399.

[37]See Frederick C. Grant, "Exegesis on Mark 7:24-30," *The Interpreter's Bible* (New York: Abingdon, 1951), 7:755.

[38]Martin Luther, in Roy A. Harrisville, "The Woman of Canaan," *Interpretation* 20:3 (July 1966), 281.

From this encounter in Mark there are several crumbs, ideas, lessons, that seem particularly appropriate for us to gather up from beneath the table and keep on this Mother's Day. There is the crumb of faith we have been talking about—the woman got what she wanted by having faith. There is the christological point: the tension within Jesus as he gathers himself for his journey toward death. Let me mention one other affirmation this text makes: the importance of telling the truth.

Jesus was surely not testing the woman, he was reflecting on his own (apparently) failing mission. She brings him up short with her response. What had she done to surprise him so? She had told the truth. And Jesus' amazement turns to admiration and delight. Perhaps he had underestimated her, but when she startles him with a truthful, penetrating response, he grants her wish and heals her daughter.

Stories like this admit of widely varying interpretation, as does much of scripture. There are people described in scripture, prophets and other religious leaders, who did not tell the truth. Interpreters have also deceived us, offering their biases as truth. Our continuing quest for the truth is difficult. But it is worth it. Writing about peace, Walter Brueggemann puts it this way:

> God promises peacemaking. This peacemaking by God only happens, however, when there is truth-telling—costly, urgent and subversive. That is the work of the church. The issue…is clear: When we lie, we die. When we speak truthfully about human reality, God sends us peace.[39]

"When we lie, we die." An unnamed Syrophoenecian mother tells the truth in her encounter with Jesus and her daughter is healed. The point is clear. We see the same thing in our time around this table. It is not a time or a place for finessing the tradition, for pretending we are other than we are. It is a time and place for telling the truth. While we were yet sinners, Christ died for us. Amazing grace. Praise God for truth-telling mothers. Praise God for the truth. Praise God for Christ.

---

[39]Walter Brueggemann, "Truth-Telling and Peacemaking," *The Christian Century* (30 Nov. 1988), 1098.

95

PENTECOST
VISIBLE TOKENS
Acts 2:1–4, 38–42

When the day of Pentecost had come, they were all together in one place....[And] those who welcomed his message were baptized, and that day about three thousand persons were added. They devoted themselves to the apostles' teaching and fellowship, to the breaking of bread and the prayers.

Dietrich Bonhoeffer was in prison in Berlin in 1943 when the day of Pentecost (Whitsunday in Europe) arrived. He began a letter to his family that Sunday which he finished on Monday. In it he said this:

> Well, Whitsuntide is here and we are still separated; but it is in a special way a feast of fellowship. When the bells rang this morning, I longed to go to church, but instead I did as John did on the island of Patmos, and had such a splendid service of my own, that I did not feel lonely at all, for you were all with me, every one of you....
>
> It is [now] Whitmonday, and I was just sitting down to a dinner of turnips and potatoes when your parcel that Rudiger brought as a Whitsuntide present arrived quite unexpectedly. I really cannot tell you what happiness such things give one. However certain I am of the spiritual bond between all of you and myself, the spirit always seemed to want some visible token of this union of love and remembrance, and then material things become the vehicle of spiritual realities. I think this is analogous to the need felt in all religions for the visible appearance of the Spirit in the sacrament.[40]

I think so, too. And I am overwhelmed by these simple but profound words from one of God's saints. A little gift in prison, a table spread in church: visible tokens of the union of love and remembrance that we have in Jesus Christ. On this day of Pentecost, when the Holy Spirit manifested itself visibly and audibly to the church, we receive these tokens of that presence with us today. May this bread and wine be the vehicle for the spiritual truth God would share with each of us today.

---

[40]Dietrich Bonhoeffer, *Letters and Papers from Prison*, ed. Eberhard Bethge (New York: Macmillan, 1967), 35–36. This text was pointed out to me by Mark Toulouse.

MEMORIAL DAY

96 THE BITTER AND THE SWEET
Revelation 10:8–11

"Take it, and eat; it will be bitter to your stomach, but sweet as honey in your mouth."

When Jesus met with the twelve and probably others to celebrate the Passover, he named two parts of their meal as symbols to remind the disciples of him—he chose bread and wine, common things. Today it seems particularly appropriate to use two other common symbols as part of our feast of remembrance. The Passover itself contains the paradox of these elements: the bitter and the sweet, bitter herb and sweet wine. The Last Supper was a bittersweet occasion—bitter with betrayal and sacrifice and death, sweet with a love that will not let us go.

This weekend, which we call "Memorial," calls to mind the bitterness of war and the sweetness of memory. We therefore partake of the memorial feast. When the bitter herb is passed, moisten your finger, touch the herb, taste and reflect on the bitterness; then eat the raisin and reflect on the sweetness, as we remember the Son of God and his sacrifice: bitter and sweet.[41]

---

[41]We used ginger for this herb. Other herbs and other sweet fruits could be used.

SUMMER

97 EVERYBODY HAS ICE...AND GRACE
Philippians 3:12–16

... this one thing I do: forgetting what lies behind and straining forward to what lies ahead, I press on toward the goal for the prize of the heavenly call of God in Christ Jesus.

summer
each warm moment calls
for the lazy richness of renewal

vacations
celebrations
yes the finest variations

from which emerges
       submerges
       converges who we really are

think of it
deliciously

long lavish drinks of leisure
to savor
>*fritter away*
>*use up*
>*spend foolishly*
> *soak up*
>*enjoy*

huge chunks of time
to taste ourselves
>*our families and friends*
>*fresh sights, experiences*

these moments given
say more of "grace" than books

these celebrations
touch the ground of worship

and in play, I think
we know that God is very much alive.[42]

The "lazy richness of renewal." What an unusual, inviting phrase! And open to much mischievous interpretation. Renewal, like resurrection, is hard work. We know that. But sometimes the impetus toward renewal emerges most vividly from the fertile perspective of quiet and leisure. I like to think of it this way. My grandmother used to say that all people were equal: "Everybody's got ice; it's just that rich folks have it in the summer and poor folks have it in the winter." Thanks a lot, Grandma. Using her image, a more helpful point might be that the difference between a burden and a luxury can be a matter of timing and perspective. Put another way, the same experience in a different setting may produce a different reaction. Ice in summer is not the same as ice in winter.

Take also what we do here at this table. In the winter of our discontent, when we are troubled, lost and lonely, this demonstration of the magnitude of God's love and grace can be the veriest salvation. As we take the bread and cup, we remember that the saving act of God in Jesus Christ reaches all the way to the pit where we find ourselves and lifts us to the higher ground of redemption.

---

[42]S. Shoemaker, "summer," in Elizabeth McMahon Jeep and Gabe Huck, *Celebrate Summer!* (New York: Paulist Press, 1973), 7.

But during the lazy, hazy days of summer, when the anxieties of life subside and souls, like the land, are sunny and warm, this communion can serve its other function: helping us to forget. We must not only remember God's saving grace, we must forget those past slights and failures that threaten to keep us from journeying gladly toward God's unfolding future. We can and must learn from the past; we must not live there. How many times I have seen persons who felt they had been injured by others, fate, or even God. They became embittered, their future calcified, their hope disappeared.

Jesus, to the very end, looked to the future, to the reign of God that was coming. What about us? Sure, we have had some hard times. Many of us have suffered beyond reason. But as the slow pace of summer gives us respite, this may be the time to put away bitterness, jealousy, anger; to forget those things which have made us less than God wants us to be; and, like Paul, to press on toward something better, to press on toward God. The lazy richness of renewal that summer affords can point us in that direction. Like Grandma said, we are all equal. We may be poor in spirit, but we are rich in Christ. So relax. Eat. Remember. Drink. Forget. Savor. Celebrate. Move on. God is very much alive.

FATHER'S DAY
98 DOING WHAT YOU HAVE TO DO
Mark 15:21–24

They compelled a passer-by, who was coming in from the country, to carry his cross; it was Simon of Cyrene, the father of Alexander and Rufus.

I have never believed that the cross was foreordained from the foundation of the world, that God told Jesus it was time to hustle on down to earth and get himself crucified. Although our track record of killing God's messengers is abysmal, I believe God hoped that this time it might be different, that Jesus would be believed and followed, not murdered. But we reacted according to form. The gospel of love fell on deaf ears and Jesus' options narrowed as he approached Jerusalem until, finally, all that was left in front of him was an old rugged cross. Being faithful to God's plan for redeeming the world and to his own vocation meant climbing up on that cross, offering himself on our behalf, and surely breaking God's heart in the process. But Jesus did what he had to do and turned an ignominious death into a vehicle for grace and salvation.

Today is Father's Day, that day when we honor dear old dad with gifts of ties and after-shave and, most importantly, hugs. It is a day when fathers perhaps sit down and look backward, considering cancelled dreams, plans for careers, and accomplishments that never happened because they put their families before themselves—it is the day when they sit back and realize they made the right decision. I think it is fitting that we remember mothers and fathers on their special days; and I have heard it said that Father's Day is like Mother's Day, except the presents are cheaper.

That may be, but I would like to offer a tribute to fathers and mothers this morning for a gift they give: that is the gift of possibility, the gift of making things possible. There is a story in the New Testament about making things possible. It is a story about a man named Simon. Although he is mentioned in Matthew, Mark, and Luke, we actually know very little about Simon. We know for sure that he was from Cyrene, the capital city of what is now Libya in North Africa, and we know that he was in Jerusalem on a Friday in about the year 30 of the common era. Most of the rest is conjecture.

Some people have claimed that Simon, coming from Africa, was black, but there is no way to know that. I think there are some things that we may, however, safely assume. I think we may assume that he was a good Jew, an observant Jew. Whether he lived in Palestine or travelled all the way from Cyrene, he had come to Jerusalem for the Passover feast, an act of dedication.

However that may be, while Simon was in the city that Friday, he noticed a commotion and, like everyone else, went to see what was happening. He saw the Romans leading three people out to be crucified. They were carrying their crosses and, just as one of them passed where Simon was standing in the crowd, the man fell and could go no farther. So it says in Mark that they compelled Simon to carry the man's cross for him. In Luke it is even stronger. It says they seized Simon and forced him to bear the burden of the cross. Why Simon...of all the people standing around? Probably for two reasons. First, he might have been, from his African dress, marked as a foreigner. For the Romans to compel a foreigner to do the dirty work of carrying the cross would have met with less resistance from the locals than having one of their own forced to do it, a kind of "wetback" mentality that is with us to this day. Or it may simply have been that Simon was a husky fellow and looked strong enough to carry the cross to the place of execution, a place called Golgotha.

We do not know how heavy the cross was, but it was heavy. We do not know how far it was to Golgotha, but it was right far, probably at least a half-mile. Can you imagine how Simon felt when the Roman pointed at him? "Oh, no! Not me! Why me?" He did not want to do it. He did not choose to do it. But he had to do it. And he did it. And the point I want to make is one seldom mentioned. Simon did what he had to do, allowed himself to experience that event in its full magnitude, and it changed his life. How do I know that? Listen.

The Gospel of Mark was written about forty years after the crucifixion of Jesus to help sustain the small Palestinian Christian community during a difficult time. It was written specifically to help them understand who they were in relation to the life, death, and resurrection of Jesus Christ. And in chapter 15 it says, "They led him out to crucify him. They compelled a passer-by…to carry his cross; it was Simon of Cyrene, the father of Alexander and Rufus." And there is the last thing we know about Simon. He was the father of Alexander and Rufus. Why would Mark mention that when none of the other writers do? For only one reason in the world. The struggling Christian community to whom Mark was writing knew Alexander and Rufus. Alexander and Rufus were likely part of the community, possibly leaders among them, and Mark mentions them to identify Simon, because everyone in the community knew the two sons and thus would be able to identify the father.

And that means that in some way lost to us Simon was profoundly affected by the experience of carrying Jesus' cross, an experience that would ultimately result in his sons becoming leaders in the early church. Was Rufus the one that Paul mentions in Romans 16:13 as "chosen in the Lord"? It is possible. Can I prove all this? No. Does it make sense. Yes. There are many things that we want to do, choose to do, ought to do—but there are many more things in this life that we simply have to do. And it is how we respond to the "have to's" of life that determine the relative joy or misery of our days. Is this knowledge not an important gift to give to our children?

No doubt Alexander and Rufus were at first ashamed that their father had to do such an awful, degrading chore as carry a cross. But because he did what he had to do with dignity and grace, and grew from the experience, you may imagine the joy and pride that would have been theirs forty years later, after old Simon was gone, when they could say, "Our dad carried the cross for Jesus."

Today we stand before that cross that Simon carried as he tracked Jesus' bleeding feet up to Golgotha. And we break bread and drink from a cup to remember Jesus' suffering and honor his willingness to offer himself on our behalf. As we do, a last image comes to mind. Phillips Brooks has been called by many the father of preaching in America. Outside of Trinity Church in Boston, where he labored for the gospel for many years, there is a statue of Brooks. Behind the statue there is another dim figure. And you have to look closely before you realize that it is Jesus—Word of the Father, now in flesh appearing. On a day when we honor fathers, both here and beyond, we should not forget the parent that stands beyond and beside us all, the Lord God Almighty, Father of heaven and earth, Mother of her people, Redeemer of the world, Spirit of goodness and truth.

Though the cause of evil prosper, yet 'tis truth alone is strong.
Though her portion be the scaffold and upon the throne be wrong.
Yet that scaffold sways the future, and behind the dim unknown,
Standeth God within the sµhadow, keeping watch above God's own.[43]

Father of our fathers, and our Father; holy faith. Faith of Jesus, faith of Simon, faith of Alexander and Rufus. We will be true to thee till death.[44]

---

[43]"One to Every Man and Nation," words by James Russell Lowell, music by Thomas John Williams.

[44]Paraphrase of "Faith of Our Fathers," words by Frederick W. Faber, music by Henri F. Hemy.

THE FOURTH OF JULY

99 GRAPES OF BLESSING
Revelation 14:9–13

"... those who worship the beast...will also drink the wine of God's wrath....Write this: blessed are the dead who from now on die in the Lord."

In 1861, Julia Ward Howe went to visit some of the federal troop encampments and she watched men sitting around the fires at night singing an old tune with some new words about "John Brown's body lying a'mouldering in the grave." Someone there challenged her to write some loftier, more dignified words for the tune. That night, back in her hotel or in a tent, we are not sure which, she awoke, picked up a pen and wrote the song we know now as "The Battle Hymn of the Republic." It was the only hymn she ever wrote, but most would settle for one hymn like that.

We need to remember that the song was written hard up against the reality of war and suffering and death. In the first stanza, she saw the Lord "trampling out the vintage where the grapes of wrath are stored." That phrase, "the grapes of wrath," entered American consciousness as an expression for trouble, for difficulty, for suffering. John Steinbeck entitled one of his greatest books *The Grapes of Wrath*. And the expression is a fitting one for the way many of us live today in this country. Worried, bitter, angry, sitting and sipping the juice from the grapes of wrath.

I was once in a country when it celebrated its independence. I have never seen such unbridled joy. Many new countries in Eastern Europe are celebrating their newly-won independence, while they remember the suffering and bloodshed that their freedom cost them. When the

Fourth of July falls on a Sunday, parallel images converge. While we are justifiably concerned about the separation of church and state and nervous about one intruding upon the other, we cannot help but ask the same question today of both our country and our faith: At what cost was our freedom purchased?

We have been richly blessed in this country. We have been even more richly blessed in our faith. As we stand before the chalice, we realize just how much. God was no doubt angry that Jesus was killed. This chalice could be brimful with the juice of anger, the grapes of God's wrath, flowing, as it says in Revelation, "as high as a horse's bridle" (14:20). But it is not. Rather, it is filled with the grapes of blessing. God has transformed the worst thing humankind ever did into a vehicle of grace. It is hard to comprehend love that profound. But here it is. And we receive it with the deepest gratitude.

AUTUMN

100 TRY TO REMEMBER: THE FESTIVAL OF MICHAELMAS
Mark 4:26–29

He also said, "The kingdom of God is as if someone would scatter seed on the ground, and would sleep and rise night and day, and the seed would sprout and grow, he does not know how. The earth produces of itself, first the stalk, then the head, then the full grain in the head.

Most everyone who has lived in New York City during the past half-century has seen the wonderful little longrunning off-Broadway show called *The Fantasticks*. The most popular song from that show and one that has become a standard for the season is "Try to Remember."

> Try to remember the kind of September
> when life was slow and oh, so mellow.
> Deep in December it's nice to remember
> the fire of September that made us mellow.[45]

It may seem strange that popular culture has produced such an evocative paean to autumn while the church has not. The fact is, however, that the church has a marvelous autumnal festival. It is called "Michaelmas."

---

[45]"Try to Remember," *The Fantasticks*, words by Tom Jones, music by Harvey Schmidt (New York: Chappell, 1960).

Unfortunately, in competition with football, it has not done well in the United States. I have always enjoyed the Michaelmas services I have attended and share the following from one of them. The first piece is the introduction to the festival; the second is the liturgy for communion, adapted from the Apostolic Tradition of Hippolytus.

> The festival of St. Michael and All Angels, or Michaelmas, is one of the so-called lesser festivals of the Christian year. Usually celebrated on September 29, it has largely disappeared from American lectionaries, but has a stronger tradition in Europe, where the fall term in many universities is still called the Michaelmas term. Michaelmas stands in polarity to Easter. If Easter is the festival of resurrection, Michaelmas is the festival of creativity. Put another way: from the vantage point of the seasons, Michaelmas is to us what Easter is south of the Equator.
>
> Michaelmas is experiencing a kind of renaissance as a festival of creativity and transformation. It reminds us that autumn has come; it is time now for "harvest home," for gathering together the experiences of the year and not just for present consumption. The seeds for the next cycle must be preserved and arranged that, through the womb-like grace of God during the incubation of the winter season, they may blossom next spring and the process of creation may continue. As poet Amanda McBroom reminds us:
>
> *Just remember in the winter*
> *far beneath the bitter snows,*
> *lies the seed that with the sun's love*
> *in the spring becomes the rose.*[46]
>
> Creativity is not the "wild spinning of fanciful minds," but the basic stuff, the foundational principle, of the universe.[47] Creativity is, to use ancient words, "Holy the Firm."[48] Some see Michaelmas as *the* festival of the coming age. While we make no such claim, we do invite everyone to participate in this festival of creativity, one of the many ways in which we may worship God. Join us as we seek to harvest the past and prepare for the future.

Seven acts of worship followed, reminiscent of the seven days of creation. These acts included scripture, poetry, dance, music, and interpretation. The sixth act was one of Eucharist.

> The Eucharistic liturgy today is adapted from the Apostolic Tradition of Hippolytus (c. 200 C.E.), one of the oldest Christian liturgies extant.[49] Using this old tradition testifies to our belief that creativity

---

[46]From "The Rose," words and music by Amanda McBroom (Secaucus, NJ: Warner-Tamerlane, 1977).

[47]See Alfred North Whitehead, *Process and Reality* (New York: The Free Press, 1978), 7, 20.

[48]See meditation #101.

[49]Our liturgy is based upon the one found in *Liturgies of the Western Church*, selected and introduced by Bard Thompson (Philadelphia: Fortress, 1980), 20-24. Used with permission.

does not mean throwing out the old for the new, but rather the creative interaction of old and new, for the vitality of both.

The tradition of Hippolytus uses one broken loaf, representing the broken body of Christ, and three cups—one filled with milk and honey, as a symbol of the food of the newborn children of God and as a token of their admission to the Promised Land; one filled with water, as a sign of the cleansing action of baptism; and the third filled with wine, as a symbol of the blood that was shed by Christ.

Words of Institution:

Celebrant: The Lord be with you.

People: And with your spirit.

Celebrant: Lift up your hearts.

People: We have them with the Lord.

Celebrant: Let us give thanks unto the Lord.

People: It is fitting and right.

Celebrant: Let us pray.

We render thanks unto you, O God, through your beloved child Jesus Christ, whom in the last times you did send to us to be a savior and redeemer and the messenger of your counsel;

• Who is your word inseparable from you, through whom you made all things and in whom you were well-pleased;

• Whom you did send from heaven into the virgin's womb and who conceived within her was made flesh and dwelt among us.

• Who fulfilling your will and preparing for you a holy people stretched forth his hands for suffering that he might release from sufferings those who have believed in you.

• Who when he was betrayed to voluntary suffering that he might abolish death and rend the bonds of the devil and tread down hell and enlighten the righteous and establish the ordinance and demonstrate the ressurection:

Taking bread and making eucharist to you said: Take, eat, this is my body which is broken for you;

Likewise also the cup, saying: This is my blood which is shed for you. When you do this, you do my anamnesis [remembrance].

And milk and honey mingled together in fulfillment of the promise which was made to the Fathers and Mothers, namely, a land flowing with milk and honey; which Christ indeed gave, even his flesh, whereby they who believe are nourished like little children, making the bitterness of the human heart sweet by the sweetness of his word;

Water also for the sign of the laver [water-basin], that the inner person also may receive the same baptismal rites as the body.

Doing therefore the anamnesis of Christ's death and resurrection we offer before you, O God, the bread and the cups, making eucharist to you. And we pray that you would grant to all who partake to be united to you that they may be fulfilled with the Holy Spirit for the confirmation of their faith in truth, that we may praise and glorify you through your beloved child Jesus Christ through whom glory and honor be unto you with the Holy Spirit in your holy church now and forever, world without end. Amen.

People: Amen.

Celebrant 1 (bread):	The bread of heaven in Christ Jesus
One who receives:	Amen.
Celebrant 2 (milk & honey):	With the promise of God
One who receives:	Amen.
Celebrant 3 (water):	By the cleansing of the Spirit
One who receives:	Amen.
Celebrant 4 (wine):	The blood of our Lord Jesus Christ
One who receives:	Amen.
Celebrant 1:	Go therefore into the world; be zealous to perform good works and to please God.

WORLDWIDE COMMUNION SUNDAY

101 HOLY THE FIRM
1 Corinthians 3:10–11; 1 Peter 1:13–16

For no one can lay any foundation other than the one that has been laid; that foundation is Jesus Christ.

… as he who called you is holy, be holy yourselves in all your conduct; for it is written, "You shall be holy, for I am holy."

Today is that day known as Worldwide Communion Sunday, that day when Christians of every creed lay down the theological weapons with which they seek to defend their own narrow portion of the truth and come to the table with every person around the world who claims Jesus as Lord and Savior. Worldwide Communion Sunday is a faint glimmer, in the midst of an almost daily more sectarian Christianity, of what Jesus meant when he said, "You must all be one."

We are literally gathered about the table this morning; in our heritage we are figuratively gathered about it every week. Why? Why this event? Why not some other event in the life of Christ? He was involved with many things that were more dramatic: his inspirational nativity, his temptation in the wilderness, his baptism, his magnificent sermon on the mount, his marvelous teaching, his stunning miracles, his triumphal entry, his ignominious crucifixion, and his glorious resurrection. All of these pack more punch than the simple, lowly Passover meal he shared with his disciples, a common meal like hundreds of others they had shared. Important as these other events are, and they have their season among us, we do not rehearse them week after week like we do when we remember and re-enact that Thursday evening supper in the upper room.

Let me suggest two reasons why I believe this celebration, this remembrance, has held such a focal point in the worship of the church for, lo, these two millennia. The first is that this table has become the foundation of our faith, because the things that it symbolizes for us are the primary things, the essential things, the things that have made us who we are as a people. This table represents God loving us enough to send Jesus to live among us, that we might behold the grace and truth of God through him. It represents Jesus loving us enough to make the ultimate sacrifice on our behalf, a sacrifice symbolized by the elements on this table. And it represents the tradition of faith that we have received: people of every race and nation, in high cathedrals and bamboo shelters, people who disagree about almost everything imaginable, but still coming to a table to proclaim faith in God. This is the foundation, and it is a firm one, one not built on sand but on the solid rock of Christ.

Paul said, "For no one can lay any foundation other than the one that has been laid; that foundation is Jesus Christ" (1 Cor 3:11). He goes on to say that the test of the firmness of a foundation is whether or not it lasts. He wrote that over nineteen hundred years ago. In the words of the old hymn:

> How firm a foundation, ye saints of the Lord,
> Is laid for your faith in his excellent word!
> What more can he say than to you he hath said,
> To you who for refuge to Jesus have fled?
>
> "The soul that on Jesus still leans for repose,
> I will not, I will not desert to its foes;
> That soul, though all hell should endeavor to shake,
> I'll never, no, never, no, never forsake."[50]

This table is the foundation of our faith: God cared; Christ sacrificed; our forefathers and mothers believed—the foundation is firm.

The second reason we come is that this table is our gateway to holiness. The root meaning of holiness is found in the separateness, the

---

[50]"How Firm a Foundation," words: "K" in Rippon's *Selection of Hymns*, 1787; early USA melody, harm. Charles Heaton, 1928.

apartness, the differentness acribed to God in the Hebrew scriptures. God is separate from us, different from us—God is holy. And the experience of the holy is overpowering and unspeakable.

Today, in the society we have created for ourselves, there is precious little opportunity to experience holiness. We work, we run, we study, we get chewed out, our refrigerator breaks down, and our hair spray does not hold up—there is not much time for the holy. And so we hold on to this table for dear life, because we know that we are gathered in an upper room with the chosen one of God and that he is breaking bread and offering it to us. At this point we learn something. We learn that the approach to holiness in the Christian faith is unique. Because holiness is not aloof, high and lifted up, separate, apart, different; suddenly we see that the experience of the holy is not reserved for the mountain top, but is to be found in the midst of life itself. What could be more common, more mundane, more everyday than supper? What is more basic than bread to eat and a cup from which to drink?[51] Jesus took an event that we do every day of our lives and he said, "Look, this is holy."

So the holiness affirmed by this table is not one of separation, but rather of connectedness. This table reminds us that our lives are not hopeless, disjointed pockets of time, but that through this table we are connected to Christ, who is our host here and, through Christ, we are connected to God. It is here that we get a fore*taste* of heaven, to be one with God and Christ, as we seek to be one with each other.

In John Steinbeck's *The Grapes of Wrath*, an old preacher named Casey puts it this way:

> "I ain't sayin' I'm like Jesus. But I got tired like Him, an' I got mixed up like Him, an' I went into the wilderness like Him, without no campin' stuff. Nighttime I'd lay on my back an' look up at the stars; morning I'd set and watch the sun come up; midday I'd look from a hill at the rollin' dry country; evenin' I'd foller the sun down. Sometimes I'd pray like I always done. On'y I coudn' figure what I was prayin' to or for. There was the hills, an' there was me, an' we wasn't separate no longer. We was one thing. An' that one thing was holy.
>
> "An' I got to thinkin', on'y it wasn't thinkin', it was deeper down than thinkin'. I got to thinkin' how we was holy when we was one thing, an' mankin' was holy when it was one thing. An' it on'y got unholy when one mis'able little fella got the bit in his teeth an' run off his own way, kickin' and draggin' and fightin'. Fella like that bust the holiness. But when they're all workin' together, not one fella for another fella, but one fella kind of harnessed to the whole shebang—that's right, that's holy."[52]

---

[51]We are all aware that, for those who are starving, supper is not the common meal it should be. That does not bely our argument. It *should* be a common occurrence and, when it is not, the world has gone wrong.

[52]John Steinbeck, *The Grapes of Wrath* (New York: Viking Press, 1972), 110.

And here on Worldwide Communion Sunday, each one of us, those of us here, those around the world, and that great cloud of witnesses, all who have ever gathered about the table and all who ever will—we all are kind of harnessed to the whole shebang, and that's right and that's holy.

We come because this experience is our foundation, and it is firm. We come because this experience opens our lives to the dimension of the holy. Let me tell you one more story. One of my favorite writers is a woman who lives alone in the San Juan Islands. Her name is Annie Dillard and she won the Pulitzer Prize for her marvelous *Pilgrim at Tinker Creek*. This summer I picked up one of her books and found something in it that fascinated me. She told a story of early Christianity and Christian thinking.

You see, in early times one of the primary tasks of the philosophers was to determine just what the universe was made of. This was well before modern chemistry. Some said air; some said water; some said fire, and so on. With the coming of Christianity, Christian philosophers entered this contest, too, and made their own assertions about the stuff that the world was made of. Do you know what they came up with? They said that there were metals, minerals, salts, and earths, but beneath it all there was another substance. It was not on the surface, so you could not see it.[53] But this basic substance at the heart of creation was in touch with the absolute; it was in touch with God. Do you see what this means? It means that the world was not fashioned by God and blindly cast into space to fend for itself. No, these old, primitive, unscientific Christians said that God never let go; that God was in touch with the basic stuff from the beginning to the end. How do we say it: "I'll never, no, never, no, never forsake." The basic substance, the basic stuff of the world is in touch with God; and the name of this substance is *Holy the Firm*.[54]

What a concept! We generally think of "firm" as down here and "holy" as up there; but no, the circle is unbroken. And did something that touched something that touched Holy the Firm, which is in touch with God, seep back into the ground water and into a vine and into a grape and into this cup? It just may have. And this symbolism brings our two concerns together at last. We come because this event, this giving, taking, and sharing of life is our foundation as a people, and it is firm. We come because this table opens us to the holiness that is in our very midst. We come because Holy the Firm reminds us of the essential

---

[53]Like the fox says to the little prince: "It is only with the heart that one can see rightly; what is essential is invisible to the eye." Antoine de Saint-Exupery, *The Little Prince* (New York: Harcourt, Brace & World, 1943), 70.

[54]See Annie Dillard, *Holy the Firm* (New York: Harper & Row, 1977), 68-69.

oneness of God and Jesus Christ and the Holy Spirit and the people of God. That's right. That's firm. That's holy.[55]

---

[55]This meditation might well lead into a song like "Take, take off your shoes, we're standing on holy ground" and, should the setting be appropriate, a discalced communion service.

102 HOCUS POCUS...BROKEN FOR YOU
1 Corinthians 11:23–26

Take, eat: this is my body, which is broken for you: this do in remembrance of me (KJV).

As we come to the table on Reformation Sunday, it is fitting to recall that it was out of the upheaval of the Reformation that came a more open table, reception of the elements in both kinds, and more freedom for personal approaches to the table.

Even so, the Reformation did not solve all the problems that surround our understanding of the meaning of this event. Martin Luther and Huldrich Zwingli struggled mightily with their theological differences at what is called the Marburg Colloquy of 1529. Luther pointed to the phrase "This is my body," to emphasize the real presence of the body and blood of Christ in the bread and wine. Zwingli pointed to "Do this in remembrance of me," to emphasize the supper as a memorial feast. While they did not reach agreement, they moved slightly toward each other, with Zwingli admitting the spiritual presence of Christ and Luther admitting that physical presence is of no benefit without faith.[56]

I certainly do not want to minimize what was, and is, at stake in that discussion. Some have done precisely that. The Latin phrase "Hoc est corpus meum" (This is my body) was corrupted into "hocus pocus," a phrase used by magicians to suggest that the sleight-of-hand used to replace one thing with another was really magic. Luther and Zwingli were debating the interpretation of 1 Corinthians 11:24b: "... this is my body which is broken for you: this do in remembrance of me" (KJV). Luther lifted up the first phrase; Zwingli lifted up the last.

I suggest we look also at the phrase in the middle: "broken for you" or "for you" in more recent translations. It seems to me that neither the presence nor the memory would be possible without the sacrifice. The substance of the elements and the kind of knowledge entailed are both subordinate to the essential truth of this feast: Christ loved us enough to

---

[56]See Roland Bainton, *Here I Stand: a Life of Martin Luther* (New York: Mentor, 1955), 249.

sacrifice himself for us, that we might have life and have it more abundantly. In the middle of our theological discussions is Christ on the cross, broken for us?

ALL HALLOW'S EVE

103 FIRSTS OR SECONDS
Joel 2:26

You shall eat in plenty and be satisfied, and praise the name of the LORD your God, who has dealt wondrously with you.

There are many places in the Bible where we read of God feeding hungry people. But there are other places where the food is not given to assuage hunger, but rather for celebration and to remind people of God's bounty. In Joel, for example, we read of threshing floors filled with grain, wine and oil vats overflowing, the people eating in plenty and satisfied.

I remember the day, when my son was small, that he learned an important new word. The word was "seconds." "May I have seconds?" He seldom wanted seconds of vegetables; desserts were another matter. We eat our firsts for hunger's sake and that of nutrition, but generally have seconds only of that which we like, that which we "celebrate."

Communion is like that. People sometimes ask me why we come to the table so often. And I guess one good answer is that we like it here. Sometimes we come for firsts, because we are hungry and need spiritual nourishment. But sometimes we come for seconds, not out of any particular great need of the moment, but just because we like it here, the community, the plenteous meaning and the overflowing memories we find about this table and celebrate with thanksgiving.

Last night there were a lot of strange creatures about in our neighborhood. I doled out the goodies to each and all. At one point later on, three "monsters" came to trick-or-treat. I gave them the candy, and then they began to laugh at me and run away. I realized what had happened. They had already been to our house once and had come back to put one over on me. What they did not know as they ran laughing into the night was that it was all right with me. Firsts or seconds, whichever you need, waiting for you at the table.

ALL SAINTS' DAY

104 ALL PRESENT AND ACCOUNTED FOR
Hebrews 12:1–2

Therefore, since we are sorrounded by so great a cloud of witnesses,
let us also lay aside every weight and the sin that clings so closely,
and let us run with perseverance the race that is set before us....

Time, someone said, is simply a way to keep everything from happening at once. And that is a good thing. If life had no orderly sequence
of events, it would not be possible. But there are exceptions to this rule,
occasions when time fades before us. Naturalist John Muir spoke of
"those great thousand-year days"[57] he experienced in the high Sierra,
and we all know how long ten seconds on a hot stove feels. Time, in
these cases, is overwhelmed in our consciousness by the events-in-time.
The same is true for the Eucharist, especially on a day like today, when
we remember and celebrate the lives of all the saints who from their
labors rest. As James Sanders has said:

> Whenever and wherever this celebration takes place the church at that
> moment is the pilgrim church arriving, just about to step over the thresh-
> old. And it is in the act of remembrance that the whole church is present
> or, as Hebrews would say, we are surrounded by "so great a cloud of
> witnesses" (12:1).[58]

At the end of the film *Places in the Heart*, this is vividly demonstrated. The scene is set in a little country church. As communion is
served, we see that all the characters, living and dead, are present to
receive the sacrament. *Everyone* is present at the table. And everyone
always is. In the words of Teilhard de Chardin:

> From the beginning of the Messianic preparation, up till the Parousia,
> passing through the historic manifestations of Jesus and the phases of
> the growth of his Church, a single event has been developing in the
> world: the Incarnation, realized in each individual, through the Eucha-
> rist.
> All the communions of a lifetime are one communion.
> All the communions of all (people) now living are one
>   communion.
> All the communions of all (people), present, past and
>   future, are one communion.[59]

Everyone else is already at the table. We wait only...for you.

---

[57]John Muir, *John of the the Mountains*, ed. Linnie Marsh Wolfe (Boston:
Houghton Mifflin, 1938), 213. See also Kent Dannen, "A Prophet Crying Aloud for
the Wilderness," (Master's Thesis, Lexington Theological Seminary, 1973), 65.

[58]James Sanders, "In the Same Night," 96.

[59]Pierre Teilhard de Chardin, *The Divine Milieu* (New York: Harper, 1960), 102.

THANKSGIVING

105 THE FEAST OF THE GREAT THANKSGIVING

Romans 6:20–23; Colossians 3:12–17

For the wages of sin is death, but the free gift of God is eternal life in Christ Jesus our Lord.

And whatever you do, in word and deed, do everything in the name of the Lord Jesus, giving thanks to God the Father through him.

We gather together again and again to celebrate what has come to be called "the feast of the great thanksgiving." Of all God's gifts to us, none is more precious than the gift of a saviour. And how thankful we are for that gift!

Thinking on the season, the gift, and the feast we share about the Lord's Table, I remembered this story from a man named Eric Sloane. Reflecting on the Bicentennial in 1976, Sloan wrote that one of the great American spirits was the spirit of thankfulness. He said:

> Once a year for the past half-century, I am reminded of a certain Thanksgiving Day dinner in a Kansas restaurant. I had run away from home to earn my way about the country as a sign-painter, and my box of paints, which also contained my worldly goods and a change of clothes, was always with me. I tucked the box under the table as I sat down. The restaurant was one of those typical, friendly small town places. The meal was memorable. When I had finished and asked for the check, the proprietor gave me a slip of paper with a penciled message. "Happy Thanksgiving," it said. "There is no charge for food on this day. We are only thankful you came by." I have long forgotten the town and the man's name, but I have carried with me that memory of graciousness for fifty years.[60]

We often emphasize the cost of the meal before us on this table, and the cost of discipleship is truly high. But the other side of the picture is that you cannot buy this meal. It is utterly free, given, as was Christ's life, unconditionally for you. It is as if, in coming to partake, we find a slip of paper which reads, "Happy Thanksgiving. There is no charge for food on this day. I am only thankful you came by." Let us eat together. And let us respond by freely and thankfully offering ourselves in Christ's service.

---

[60]Eric Sloane, *The Spirits of '76* (New York: Walker, 1973), 32.

Contemporary

CONTEMPORARY

106 RE/MEMBER

The word "remember" is central to the celebration of Holy Communion. Some form of the word is carved into communion tables around the world and it is found in every liturgy for those tables. Some time ago, however, I heard a preacher say "the opposite of remember is not forget; the opposite of remember is dismember."[1] I was disoriented by that assertion and thought about it for a long time. Certainly one could make the case that remembering and forgetting are opposites. However, "the opposite of remember is dismember" opens a new door of understanding for us. When intending this meaning of the word, I have chosen to write "re/member" with a slash, allowing the more common meaning to maintain its own integrity.

Coming to the table together in this light is an act of re/membering, of being put back together, of being made right. The Greeks had a word, *apokatastasis*, which hints at this, that eventually everything will be made right, that all of creation, now hopelessly sundered and fractious, will be restored to peace and harmony.

Our gathering here is an anticipation of that time. When the centrifugal force of life in this world threatens to dismember us, it is here that we remember Jesus and are re/membered by him into the living Body of Christ. So our partaking is not only, as we perhaps thought, a solitary act; it is also an act of community-building. And what a community it is! God, Jesus, Holy Spirit, you, the ones on either side of you, everyone gathered here today, all those gathered about the table of Jesus Christ everywhere in the world, all those who have ever partaken of the Supper and all those who ever will…are re/membered, are ONE in this moment. If we believed and acted upon this utterly true statement of faith, what a difference it could make in the world!

There are so many. It will take a little while to serve everyone. But we have time. As we come to the table this morning, I invite you to think of someone you would like to have with us at the table today; it may be someone who is a long way away from us today, someone who has gone on before, someone you have never met but would like to meet, someone who has not even been born yet. Name them in your heart, and invite them to come and be part of this community today. For my part, I

---

[1]From a sermon by Rita Nakashima Brock. See note #48. I do not know if the affirmation is original with her.

name the name of Bill Shelly. Come. Let us remember. Come. Let us be re/membered as the people of God. Jesus is waiting to put us back together again.

107   COMMUNION AND COMMUNITY

Once upon a time food was a central ingredient in community. People did much sharing with each other as they gathered about the table. But, as Henri Nouwen has written, "it seems that food has lost the power to create community."[2] Perhaps that is because once upon a time food was hard to come by and received with appreciation and thanksgiving. Nowadays food is taken for granted by a large percentage of us. Only when health concerns change our diets or when we see starving people on television do we think much about it. The family dinner table and the conversation there often loses out to the pressure of work and other activities.[3]

In the face of such lost concern and conversation comes W. H. Auden's reminder: "Hunger allows no choice to the citizen or the police; we must love one another or die."[4] This heightens for me even more than usual the importance of what we do about this table. Jesus gathered his friends and, as his last act of fellowship with them, he fed them, he asked them to be one with him and each other, he asked them to remember him. And we must cling tenaciously to this table; we must not let it or its significance be lost to us or to our children. Here we feed on spiritual food and we do it together, perhaps one of the last best hopes that we have of being the united community that Jesus wanted us to be.

---

[2]Henri Nouwen, *Reaching Out* (Garden City: Doubleday, 1975), 16.
[3]See also meditation #119.
[4]W. H. Auden, "September 1, 1939" in *Modern British Poetry*, ed. Louis Untermeyer (New York: Harcourt, Brace & World, 1958), 462.

108   FROM THE BOTTOM

Here are two stories from Fred Craddock and Carlyle Marney. Craddock, reminiscing about a time in his youth, said that during one particularly inspiring moment of worship, the question was asked, "Are ye able to drink this cup… ?" He responded, "Yes, I am able to drink the cup." They handed it to him and he did not drink it down. Rather, he said, "I have been sipping it for forty years."[5] Many of us can identify with that.

Marney, before he died, wrote that many years before he had heard that a pastor friend of his was dying and that he was going to preside at his last worship service that Sunday. Marney went and when it was time for communion, people went forward and knelt, as was the custom in that church. Marney was the last one in line. When his old friend, now dying on his feet, came to him, there was little wine left in the chalice. He gave it to Marney to drink and then, as he turned and walked back to the altar, Marney watched him stop and turn the chalice up to get the last ruby drop himself. He took his last drink from the bottom of the cup.[6]

Generally, we sip from the cup of salvation, just enough nourishment to get us through the week. But from time to time we need to remind ourselves how total was the sacrifice of Jesus Christ and how total is the commitment that he asks of us. Take the cup of blessing and, as a reminder, drink it…from the bottom.

---

[5]Remembered from a sermon by Craddock many years ago.
[6]See Marney, *The Crucible of Redemption*, 55-56.

109   CONGEALED COMMUNION

Stephan Farris tells a story about a young pastor who arrived at his first church.[7] He went into the kitchen on Saturday night to prepare the elements for Sunday morning communion. He cut the loaf into bite-sized pieces. He found no grape juice but, rammaging through the cupboard, he found a can of grape powder. Assuming this was what the congregation used, either by choice or financial necessity, he mixed a pitcherful, tasted it, and found it palatable. He poured the juice into the

---

[7]Stephan Farris teaches at Knox College, Toronto, Ontario, Canada.

trays of little cups and then put the bread and cups into the refrigerator for the night.

The next morning the assigned deacon placed the elements on the table and, at the proper time, the new minister moved to the table and intoned the words of institution. The elders prayed and the elements were distributed to the people.

The minister sat, head bowed in prayer, behind the table. After a while, he stole a glance at the congregation and was stunned to find everyone, including the deacons with the trays, looking at him.

The cups were filled with grape Jello!

I did not hear what happened next. But I wonder. Was Christ present for those people in the Jello? Or in the Fritos and Coca-Cola of a youth group Eucharist? Or in the grapes and ginger of a retreat communion? I could not tell them no. For Christ continues to meet us, sometimes in extraordinary ways, in the midst of our ordinariness.

110   TAIZÉ THOUGHTS FOR THE TABLE

The monastic community at Taizé in France was founded by Roger Schutz and three brothers in the 1940s. It was to be an ecumenical community where the focus was on reconciliation and compassionate love among people. Called the "springtime" of the Church by John XXIII, Taizé grew to be an important center for those, especially young people, who were seeking to get in touch with God, their faith, and others.[8] Breaking bread together is an important part of life at Taizé. In the Rule of Taizé is this description of the meal:

> Each meal should be an agape in which our brotherly love is manifest in joyfulness and simplicity of heart.
>
> The occasional moments of silence at mealtime bring you refreshment when you are weary or communion in prayer for the companion who partakes of the same bread.
>
> Let the brother whose task it is to wait upon the table facilitate the peace of the meal by his watchfulness.[9]

There are at least five images in this beautiful rule that would enrich our circle about the communion table. Think about each one as I say it:

---

[8]See Peter C. Moore, *Tomorrow Is Too Late* (London: A. R. Mowbray, 1970) and Rex Brico, *Taize': Brother Roger and His Community* (London: Collins, 1978).

[9]From "The Rule of Taize,'" in *Unity Trends*, 1 April 1969, p. 6.

joyfulness, simplicity of heart, refreshment of silence, prayer for our companions, watchfulness. Each of these is not only inherent in what we do at this table, richly present and available now, but each is something we desperately need. There is so much sorrow, so much complexity, so much noise, so little prayer, so little awareness in our daily lives. Perhaps the experience of these blessings can teach us something and hasten the day when this service will be a reflection of the sacrificial way we live and not the opposite.

111 MORE TAIZÉ THOUGHTS FOR THE TABLE

One of the great contributions the Taizé community has made to the universal church has been that of liturgical renewal. The heart of community life is the celebration of the Sunday Eucharist. It is a time, according to one brother, for prayer, for remembering Christ, for joining Christ, for receiving Christ, for becoming one with all the church.[10]

The service begins with prayer, followed by scripture, song, and sermon. The Eucharist proper consists of offering, of prayer, of bread and wine. Peter C. Moore describes the closing of the service this way:

> The Communion is distributed in silence. All go back to their places for a prayer of thanksgiving and the dismissal. There is nothing more to be done or said but to return to ordinary life of which worship is an extraordinary part, recalling the Prior's words that God seems more often absent than present during times of prayer; but this is no worry to him. "It is not at the time of prayer, but afterwards that God is known."[11]

Think on these two ideas as we approach the table today. The first is silence. We have so little of it and are therefore so uncomfortable with it. But silence is at the heart of the religious impulse. God...and silence. Our liturgies and services are but picture frames around the vast, deep silence of God.

Secondly, our approach to the table is sometimes demanding and all wrong. We may insist that God provide us with all God's spiritual benefits right now. But they seldom come that way. Often, as Brother Roger says, it is later that God becomes known to us. The call to the table for Christians is a many-splendored thing. Two of the splendors we must not forget are silence and patience.

---

[10]Moore, 70.
[11]Moore, 75.

112   PLASTIC BREAD

It came in the mail this week. Another in a long line of pleas for money to help a cause. This one included a little plastic loaf of bread with a slot in the top where one could put money. This is no commentary on the cause involved, but they used the wrong symbol for me. Plastic bread. Ugh! The worst part is that it is not that much different from the bread we get in stores these days. Looks and tastes like wallpaper paste. I consider myself both fortunate and woebegone that I may belong to the last generation that remembers real bread. When my grandmother made bread, I had to leave the house. The aroma drove me to Pavlovian distraction. And fresh farm butter on bread hot from the oven— that may be as close to heaven as we can get in this world. I once heard a story about poor people in heaven. Many of the wonders of the celestial city did not impress them. What they were most moved by was neither the architecture nor the music. It was the bread. Something special, it was. Real, wonderful bread.

The bread we are getting ready to eat, to be honest, is not much. Not warm. Almost tasteless. But it does have something special, something that makes it real. It has a memory. A memory of a sacrifice made by Jesus that we might live. A dedication to follow in his footsteps. A resolve to share this living bread with all the world. As we come to the table, think on the things that make this bread real for all who believe in Jesus Christ.

113   THE HEAVIEST CROSS

The protagonist in Ralph Ellison's *Invisible Man* descends into a New York City subway, where this striking scene occurs:

> A train came. I [entered and] stood, holding onto the center pole, looking down the length of the car. On one side I saw a white nun in black telling her beads; across the aisle there was another dressed completely in white, the exact duplicate of the other except that she was black and her black feet bare. Neither of the nuns was looking at the other but at their crucifixes, and suddenly I laughed and a verse I'd heard long ago paraphrased itself in my mind:
>
> > *Bread and Wine,*
> > *Bread and Wine,*
> > > *Your cross ain't nearly so*
> > > *Heavy as mine....*[12]

_____

[12]Ellison, 43

The contrast and irony are striking. Black, white, white, black, pain all around. The lamentation "is there any pain like mine?" is real. "Minor surgery" is always performed on others. Two things, I think, can help us here. One is to work at being sensitive to the pain of others. The other is to see all suffering in light of the One who suffered supremely. The heaviest cross was the one laid across Jesus' back, for the sins of the world were piled on top of the spiked wood. If we begin by saying, "Bread and Wine, Bread and Wine: Jesus' cross was heavier than mine," then perhaps we can be more loving and caring toward one another.

114   AN UNUSED CUP

I am an unused communion cup,
    left from last Sunday's service,
Giving mute testimony to an appointment unkept—
    a trust broken.
I was filled in anticipation that some Christian
    would drink of my contents and be reminded
    of the price of his or her redemption.
Here I sit...unused.
Yet I bear witness of a love extended,
    a fellowship desired,
    a grace made available.
"This is the new covenant in my blood."
Here I remain...reminding one and all
    that God's gifts must be claimed.
God forces neither Godself nor God's blessings
    on anyone, but eagerly awaits acceptance.[13]

This little piece, copied from an old church newsletter, reminds me of one of the basic rules of the faith community: we have to get together. One can have faith as an ascetic alone in the desert, but one cannot have a faith community. Yes, the church is within you, but not you alone. We need each other. More than just an hour is lost when we choose not to be in worship, not to be at the table. Church, for better or worse, is where the Christian faith becomes credible. Too many unused cups create a credibility gap that grows harder and harder to bridge. It is very good to see you here at the table today. Take care for those you do not see here, and remind them how much we miss them!

---

[13]Copied and adapted from *The Chimes*, a newsletter of the State Street Christian Church, Redlands, CA, 11 Feb. 1982. I do not know the original source.

115   BAD EATING HABITS[14]

We are witnessing today an explosion of bad eating habits in North America. Some do not have enough food; many have too much. Too many complain about food that people elsewhere would be grateful to have. Those who have plenty often eat the wrong things—out of sloth, ignorance, or a misguided perception of what they need to make them attractive or strong. Anorexia and bulimia stretch toward epidemic levels, especially among our young people. I remember seeing an article about a beautiful young actor named Alexandra Paul. Politically involved and candid about her own problems, she tells young people: "The next time you see me on the screen and think I'm so perfect, remember I've leaned over a toilet bowl and stuck my finger down my throat."[15]

Eating and drinking habits, once engrained, are very hard to break. Let me suggest a good habit, which might even help with some of the bad ones. Communion. The more we come to the table of Jesus Christ and take the loaf and cup in memory of him, the more we realize how much he really loves us, and the less we will want to ruin the precious gift of our lives. This tiny bit of food is not magic; it will not make us sexy. But it can help us become more spiritually healthy, and that is the touchstone to becoming a healthier whole person.

Alexandra Paul knows that she is not perfect. Neither are we. But she is dearly loved by God. And so are we.

---

[14]This meditation is written with young people especially in mind.
[15]Alexandra Paul, in "Dragnet . . . ," *People Weekly* 28:4 (27 July 1987), 59.

116   BLOODY RELIGION

A person came up to me once and said, "I'm sure glad our church doesn't have a bloody religion like some of the others." Well, we do not talk about it much, but we do have a bloody religion. The body and blood of Christ, broken and poured out that we might have life. I remember a hymn from my youth. It was hard for me to sing without getting queasy: "There is a fountain filled with blood, drawn from Immanuel's veins."[16] It almost makes Jesus sound like a blood donor. And there is something to be said for that image.

---

[16]"There Is a Fountain Filled with Blood," words: William Cowper, music: Lowell Mason.

In a course I teach on spiritual disciplines, one of the contemporary disciplines we study is that of giving blood. It is one of the very real ways in which we can share in God's work of giving life. At the Carter Blood Center in Fort Worth, they share these thoughts from a blood drive chairperson:

> I'm giving my blood.
> Christ already gave his.
>> I'll give a meager pint.
>> Christ gave his all.
> My needle was small, sharp and sterile.
> His nails were large, dull and surely unclean.
>> My table is soft, comfortable.
>> His cross was rough, painful.
> My attendants are gentle, kind.
> His soldiers were harsh, cruel.[17]

The contrast is vivid. And it becomes even more so now that the giftlike nature of blood has come into question. LeAnn Griffin, after visiting the blood center, wrote this:

> Blood seems so mysterious. A beautiful, organic color.
> Blood enlivens us—mobilizes us—flushes us—carries us—
> frightens, sickens, surprises us. The double-edged gift.
> If blood is life, we're afraid of losing it. In the 1990s
> blood is death and we are afraid to share or to receive it.
> I've always heard 'tis better to give than to receive, but
> it's harder to receive than to give.[18]

And it is hard to come to this table to receive the elements of Christ's sacrifice for us. Why? Because thinking about what he did for us makes us think about what we have done for him—and for most of us, it is not nearly enough. Two things we need: an acceptance of the grace that comes to us in spite of everything, and a commitment to be the church—to be the body of Christ in this place and time.

---

[17]"Thoughts from a Blood Drive Chairperson," Author unknown, from the Carter Blood Center, Fort Worth, Texas.

[18]LeAnn Griffin, Class journal for HOWO 7243, Brite Divinity School, Fort Worth, Texas, Summer, 1989.

117   COSMIC COMMUNION

There is a marvelous place on Whidbey Island off the coast of Washington called the Chinook Learning Community. All kinds of people from all kinds of religious traditions come there. I have been there several times on retreat and have never failed to come away refreshed and renewed. One of their traditions is the Sunday morning celebration of the Eucharist. On one occasion I sat next to a Jew who partook of the elements of Communion for the first time in his life.

How could he do so? Only because Chinook's understanding of Christ tends to differ from that held by most of us. While my view of Christ is inextricably tied to the incarnation of Christ in Jesus of Nazareth, the Chinook vision is more cosmic in nature. Remembering Jesus' promise that "where two or three are gathered together in my name, there I am," teachers in the Chinook tradition say "From twos and threes and fours and fives we build towards a world of several million souls, indeed billions of souls, all of whom can be meshed together in time, in this vast communion of life."[19] Thus, as Jesus' life of love, service, and divinity becomes manifest in us, Christ-consciousness grows and spreads.

Speaking with some ministers later, I indicated my skepticism about such a cosmic Christ, expecting they would all agree with me. One replied, "What's wrong with a cosmic Christ? What's wrong with an understanding of Christ that transcends our own little claims about him?" I had to think about that. I have not been back to Chinook in some time. But if nothing else remains of that experience for me, this does. To J. B. Phillips' well-known warning that "Your God is too small," I now have to add the danger that our Christ is too small.

At this table more than anywhere else, we are reminded just how large the gift of Jesus Christ was and is. As we take these elements to remember him, we do so knowing that we remember but a portion, that we have so much left to learn, and rejoicing in the promise that someday we shall see him face to face.

---

[19]David Spangler, *Reflections on the Christ* (The Park, Scotland: Findhorn Lecture Series, 1977), 19-20.

118 THE PROPER TIME FOR BREAKING BREAD Part I

King David Cole is a great Kansas City preacher. Reflecting recently on his childhood in Arkansas, he described his most vivid memory of those long-ago Sunday mornings. He and his sister had the job of taking to church the communion bread that his grandmother had baked.

David remembered that the bread was nicely wrapped in a napkin for the journey; he also remembered that he and his sister frequently would get into squabbles with each other along the way. They were not mature enough yet to move beyond these sibling tiffs, but they were always careful to set the bread safely aside before fighting with each other. They knew that the bread was to be broken in church by the elder at the table, but they also knew it had better not be broken before then. Somehow, even in their childishness, they knew that the communion service had something to do with time, with proper time.[20]

Jesus was born at the proper time. When it was time, he set his face toward Jerusalem. At precisely the right time in God's economy of salvation, he broke bread and was broken for us. Why is the bread not broken beforehand, on the way to church or in the kitchen? Because the breaking is as important as the bread, the action is as important as the substance. Christ once became known to two friends, not in the bread they ate, but in the breaking of it. So, like David and his sister, always be careful with the bread. It is time now to break it, and this may be just the right moment for you. Today, as we commune together, may Christ become known to you in the breaking of the bread.

---

[20]Remembered from a story told by King David Cole at the Red River Preaching Workshop, Lake Murray, Oklahoma, 29 May 1991.

119 THE PROPER TIME FOR BREAKING BREAD Part II

Sometimes people ask me why our celebration of the Lord's Supper is kept until the very end of our worship service. In one sense I cannot answer, because it was that way when I came to this church, and I am not sure about the reasoning of the people who put it there.

I know that in the church where I grew up it was early in the service until the preacher changed it, because the deacons had developed the pattern of serving communion and then going across the street to the coffee shop during the sermon. And the preacher did not like that.

But I do not think that was the major reason. I turned on the television yesterday just long enough to hear the sportscaster say that the Houston Astros were only six outs away from winning the National League pennant. But I looked in the paper this morning and read that the Philadelphia Phillies had won the game. They say the game is not over until the last person is out…and here, for us, the service is not over until the last person is served.

Communion reminds us of God's love and Jesus' sacrifice, and it is appropriate that this be on our minds as we leave. We have saved it until last because it is the most important, and because it is the best. Come to the table and enjoy the benefits and the challenges of the loaf and cup.

120   THE SPACE OF THE SUPPER

I have thought often about the "time" of the Supper (as witnessed by the two previous meditations), but I had never thought about the "space" of the Supper, at least not before I heard art historian Leo Steinberg give a lecture entitled "It Takes Years to Look at a Picture." In that lecture Steinberg said, "Art historians have a tremendous sense of space but no sense of time whatsoever."[21] He then spent the better part of a very interesting hour speaking about the position of Jesus' hands in Leonardo da Vinci's painting *Last Supper*. I later read a more detailed analysis by Steinberg. He suggested seven (!) functions of the hands of Christ in the painting:

> (1) Christ spreads his hands in to express willing surrender; (2) the gesture accuses the traitor; (3) it contours Christ's shape so as to allude to the Trinity; (4) both hands together, pointing to bread and wine, evoke the sacrament of communion; (5) the open hand, defining the radius of the church dome, extends the promise of life to the sleeping dead; (6) the palms, alternately prone and uplifting, prefigure the Judge of the Second Coming.[22]

It is, however, the seventh function that is the most fascinating. The perspective of the painting is ambivalent. On the intellectual level, we see a rectangular room. On a more visionary level, the convergence of

---

[21]Leo Steinberg, lecture given at Texas Christian University, Fort Worth, TX, 13 April 1989.

[22]Steinberg, "The Seven Functions of the Hands of Christ: Aspects of Leonardo's *Last Supper*," in *Art, Creativity and The Sacred*, ed. Diane Apostolos-Cappadona (New York: Crossroad, 1985), 55. I am indebted to Shari Gouwens for making this article available to me.

the walls (which cannot meet except at infinity!) charge the scene with divine influence. In Steinberg's words:

> Leonardo makes actual space seem contingent on the divine presence. Christ's arms anticipate and embrace the *real* perspective. All visible space is defined in his aura, and perspective itself becomes sanctified. Christ, the submissive Christ of the Passion, literally imparts himself to the world. He moves his hands—no more than that; and at his motion, the very order of space, the laws governing visibility, are revealed as a divine emanation.[23]

I am all but rendered mute by Steinberg's ability to see so much in the slight, frozen action of Jesus' hands at the table. I thought it was a nice painting, but goodness, it really must take years to see a picture! Three quick lessons, though, that even I can see. First, I am glad there are people like Steinberg who work to help us see more clearly. Second, I am challenged to be more intentional with what I am given to see.[24] And third, there is so much to be learned from this simple memorial meal, which took place not only in time but also in space. What do the original space of the upper room and the space where we meet today have in common? How can we become better "seers" of the sacred spaces of our lives? And how does *where* we are shape *who* we are? So many new questions. God grant us growing understanding and a measure of peace in the midst of our ever-so-partial knowledge. This much is for sure: not just the time, but also the space, of this simple meal, is charged with the presence of Christ! Alleluia!

---

[23]*Ibid.*, 59.

[24]One aid to better seeing is Annie Dillard's marvelous *Pilgrim at Tinker Creek* (New York: Bantam, 1975), which contains this delightful, and insightful, paragraph on p. 16: "It is still the first week in January, and I've got great plans. I've been thinking about seeing. There are lots of things to see, unwrapped gifts and free surprises. The world is fairly studded and strewn with pennies cast broadside from a generous hand. But—and this is the point—who gets excited by a mere penny? If you follow one arrow, if you crouch motionless on a bank to watch a tremulous ripple thrill on the water and are rewarded by the sight of a muskrat kit paddling from its den, will you count that sight a chip of copper only, and go your rueful way? It is dire poverty indeed when [people are] so malnourished and fatigued that [they] won't stoop to pick up a penny. But if you cultivate a healthy poverty and simplicity, so that finding a penny will literally make your day, then, since the world is in fact planted in pennies, you have with your poverty bought a lifetime of days. It is that simple. What you see is what you get."

121   TABLE TALK

A generation ago, a sociologist said: "The one single most important factor in a child's development is his father's conversation at the dinner table."[25] We would surely use different language now, in recognition of changing roles and the fact that not all children grow up in families where two parents and children sit down together for family meals. Nevertheless, I still claim one all-but-lost affirmation of Ligon's and that is the value of conversation about the table.

Some time back I was preaching in Fort Smith, Arkansas, and, along with several others, was invited to the home of the venerable Will Sessions for breakfast. At most of the meals I have eaten in my life, the food was primary, the conversation incidental. But not this one. After the table was spread and thanks returned, Will announced the topic of conversation for the meal, initiated the discussion, and then moderated the conversation, making sure that everyone at the table had the opportunity to contribute. It was wonderful. And the food was good, too.

Thinking about the meal we share at this table, I realize that some prefer silence and privacy during communion, and I understand that. But I also suggest that the words, thought and spoken, that surround this meal can make a real difference in how we partake. One of the Gospels lends support here, for as Paul Minear says of Luke: "the center of gravity shifts from the Supper itself to the sayings after the Supper."[26] I appreciate the words from scripture, from the great traditions of the church, from those who preside intentionally and creatively. And someday I would like to see this happen: the table is spread, thanks are returned, the topic of conversation announced, and people invited to share with one another what this service of remembrance means to them. I think that would be wonderful. And the food would be good, too.

---

[25]Ernest Ligon, cited by Rhodes Thompson in a sermon preached for the Regional Assembly of the Christian Church (Disciples of Christ) in the Southwest at University Christian Church, Fort Worth, Texas, 21 October 1984.

[26]Paul S. Minear, "A Note on Luke xxii:36," *Novum Testamentum* 7:2 (1964), 129.

122 OTHER BLOODS: JESUS CHRIST AND GOD'S MIDDLE CHILDREN[27]
Genesis 1:20–25; Acts 8:26–35

And God said, "Let the earth bring forth living creatures of every kind...."And it was so....And God saw that it was good.

So Philip ran up to it and heard him reading the prophet Isaiah. He asked, "Do you understand what you are reading?" He replied, "How can I, unless someone guides me?" And he invited Philip to get in and sit beside him. Now the passage of scripture that he was reading was this: "Like a sheep that was led to the slaughter, and like a lamb silent before its shearer, so he does not open his mouth."

My brothers and sisters. Some of you are the firstborn of your parents: the "peg o' your mama's heart" and the "apple of your daddy's eye," the one in whom the family hopes—and the burden of the family heritage—are vested. Some of you are the lastborn of your parents: the beloved baby of the family, fawned over, doted upon, spoiled, the one who could do no wrong.

The rest of you...were born somewhere in the middle. Traditional psychology tells us that middle children often must struggle to receive enough affection, and that they sometimes suffer from a lack of attention.[28] One thing is certain. Barring tragedy, the children of the middle never know what it is to be an only child, to receive the complete attention of her or his parents. There is just always somebody else there.

In the beginning God created the heavens and the earth. At the climax of creation, we like to read it, God created humankind, male and female created God them. In the *middle* God created the birds of the air and the fish of the sea and everything that creepeth upon the ground, each according to its own kind. God saw that it was good. But nobody asked the animals if they thought the order of creation was good: caught in the middle—ravaged by both the capricious nature of the earth and the indifference and cruelty of humankind—always searching and yet never since creation knowing what it is to be an only child of God. In the movie "Oh God!" George Burns said that God was leaving for awhile to visit with animals. High time!

One of the dangers that we face in preaching is that someone will hear. On Ash Wednesday I sat in this chapel and heard the preacher say:

---

[27]Sermon preached at community worship, School of Theology at Claremont, 13 Apr. 1983.

[28]See Lucille K. Forer, *Birth Order and Life Roles* (Springfield, IL: Thomas, 1969).

In this season of penitence and wandering, I ponder ceaselessly the sin of looking at everything from the human perspective... some call it "narrow anthropocentrism." When will we be able to relate to the world in a manner that expresses our wonder of its beauty, integrity and harmony within the whole of God's creation and of the function and responsibility of the human species? The mark of the ashes on my forehead says that I am brooking over these tragedies, mysteries and anticipations.[29]

Oh, how I heard that...and I have not gotten rid of it yet. Think of what we have to learn. There is so much that we can learn from, and experience with, God's middle children. Animals are beautiful. They possess a grace of movement and a freedom of spirit that we cannot match. Unlike people, animals are comfortable with their bodies, not always trying to change them to conform with some faddish idea about what is attractive. Children often receive their first lessons in wonder and grief by experiencing the birth and death of animals.

And other lessons, like trust, exuberance, and responsibility develop out of the relationship between human and other animals. Matthew Fox calls animals one of our pathways to compassion. And he is right.[30] We can "gentle" our lives through contact with them.

But there is something else to consider here. Everything I have just said defines nonhuman animals in human terms. And, nice as it is, it remains narrow, anthropocentric, and speciesist. I believe that nonhuman animals are just as much God's children as we are. They do not exist solely for our benefit or pleasure. They exist because God made them according to their own kind and saw that it was a good piece of work. They are different from us, and our seeking to imbue them with human characteristics does them and Creation a disservice. That great, bored bear at the San Diego Zoo who waves to busloads of tourists as they roll by his grotto is not nearly so cute in my mind as he is exploited.

Sometimes when I used to call my cat, Blue, he would run to me, and I liked that. But sometimes when I called him, he would look at me and then slowly turn and walk away, informing me quite plainly: "Listen, Jeter. Just because you feed and shelter me, you think you own me. But you don't. I'm my own creature. And in my own soul I have something that you probably never will: the freedom to be what I am." For some reason I liked that, too.

So, you ask me, if nonhuman animals are so different from us, why are you preaching this to us? No squirrels or turkeys here today! I am preaching this to you because I do not have the gifts that Jesus and Francis

---

[29]C. Dean Freudenberger, "Penitential Markings," a sermon preached at community worship, School of Theology at Claremont, 16 Feb. 1983.

[30]Lecture given by Matthew Fox to the Southwest Association of Christian Church Educators, Athens, Texas, February, 1977.

had. I cannot communicate the way they did. All I can do is talk to you. All I can do is ask if it bothers you that one species *per day* is becoming extinct on this planet. Some of the animals you show your children at the zoo, they will not be able to show their children, because they will be gone.

Out on the corner by the administration building flies the flag of this state, which was once called the Bear Flag Republic. On that flag is a grizzly bear, the state animal of California. Does it bother you that the last wild grizzly bear in this state was killed over sixty years ago? Do you know of another state whose state animal is extinct within that state? And does it bother you that Big Bear, the resort area a few miles to the east of us, was once a veritable paradise for bears until hunting parties came in to see how many they could kill just for the fun of it? They killed them all.[31] Does it bother you? Well, it bothers me, and it brings me to understand why the great John Muir once wrote: "If a war of races should occur between the wild beasts and Lord Man, I would be tempted to sympathize with the bears."[32]

In one of God's larger lapses of judgment, God gave us, the babies of creation, dominion over our nonhuman brothers and sisters, and we have failed quite miserably in the assignment. John Cobb once said that the only thing that has intrinsic value is experience. So when we support factory farms that keep calves penned up in the dark all their short lives, with no freedom of movement, and feed them a special diet designed to make them anemic—all so their veal will be white… ; when we debeak chickens and cage them so tightly that they cannot move, cannot in fact do anything but eat and excrete… ; when we ordain that millions upon millions of nonhuman animals each year have utterly no reason to exist except to be slaughtered…what are we saying about the value of their lives?[33]

Maybe part of our problem is that we keep asking the wrong question. "Do they have a soul?" is not the right question. Nor is "can they reason?" or "can they talk?" In a different context Jeremy Bentham put the right question two centuries ago: "Can they suffer?"[34]

Think on that question and then consider these:

Can we not do better?

Can we not exchange our hunting rifles for cameras and binoculars and journals? As Roger Caras put it, "Hunting is an absurd anachro-

---

[31]See Tracy I. Storer and Lloyd P. Tevis, Jr., *California Grizzly* (Lincoln, NE: Univ. of Nebraska Press, 1978), especially chps. 8 & 11.

[32]John Muir, *A Thousand-Mile Walk to the Gulf* (Boston: Houghton-Mifflin, 1917), 122.

[33]See Stephen C. Rose, "An Ethic of Eating and Drinking," *The Christian Century* 99:16 (5 May 1982), 527.

[34]Jeremy Bentham, in Peter Singer, *Animal Liberation* (New York: Avon, 1975), 8.

nism, a leftover, a shard of a buried culture, an unwelcome artifact of another kind of man."[35] Big game hunter Theodore Roosevelt was once regaling John Muir with the joys of the manly sport of hunting. Muir's response was choice: "Mr. President, grow up."[36]

Can we not begin to consider more mindful habits of diet and apparel? A change in our habits would be better for both human and nonhuman animals. There would be more grain to feed hungry people. And there would be healthier people overall. It has occurred to me that heart attacks may be cattle's revenge! We have rediscovered soup at our house—primarily out of economic necessity—but partly out of a raised consciousness.

And can we not put the rights of nonhuman animals somewhere on our list of concerns? Not at the top, but at least on the list. Can we not protest the brutal treatment of nonhuman animals in research and food-raising operations? And can we not support those dedicated environmental organizations who are working to preserve the lives and the habitats of our elder brothers and sisters? Because once they are gone, they are gone forever.

Where would that leave us? In words attributed to Chief Seattle, "What are we without the beasts? If all the beasts were gone, we would die from a great loneliness of spirit. For whatever happens to the beasts, soon happens to us. All things are connected."[37]

All things are connected. I begin to understand more clearly what we are about in this place. Paraphrasing C.S. Lewis:

> One of the singular characteristics of our species is our yearning to know other bloods, not out of curiosity but because we have a desperate need to recognize them as our peers and because we are delighted and comforted by innocent association with other of God's

---

[35]Roger Caras, "Are We Right in Demanding an End to Animal Cruelty?" in *On the Fifth Day: Animal Rights & Human Ethics*, edd. Richard Knowles Morris and Michael W. Fox (Washington, D.C.: Acropolis, 1978), 135.

[36]Paraphrased from Muir. See Linnie Marsh Wolfe, *Son of the Wilderness: The Life of John Muir* (Madison: Univ. of Wisconsin Press, 1978), 292.

[37]When this sermon was first preached in 1983, I assumed this to be a true quotation from Chief Seattle. I had it from Paula M. Whitmore, "Reflections on the Place of Creatures," *Riverside Christian* 32:6 (10 August 1982), 2. Since that time I have learned that Chief Seattle never said these words. They were put into his mouth by a screenwriter in 1972. See "Just Too Good to Be True," *Newsweek* (4 May 1992), 68. I have left the statement in the sermon with the disclaimer "attributed to," because I liked it and because, as Herman Viola, an expert on American Indian history, said in the *Newsweek* article, Chief Seattle's mythical speech "conveys the feeling a lot of Indians had. There *was* some Indian out there who would have said that kind of thing." I have, however, learned from this. The lesson here, for me and all of us, involves the necessity of a certain "hermeneutics of suspicion" about remarks that are "too good to be true."

creatures. Because we believe ourselves to be above the rules and rhythms of nature, an un-natural animal, we have been the loneliest of animals, confused about our origins and divorced from the company of our peers.[38]

And this clinches it. A man named Bil Gilbert once travelled thousands of miles to a remote island outpost south of Australia. The island is Tasmania, and on that island and nowhere else in the world lives an endangered animal that we have named the Tasmanian devil. Gilbert went to find one. They are seldom seen anymore, and Gilbert's quest was difficult. Finally, after weeks of stalking around in the night looking for the creature, it happened. When the animal moved into the dim light that been set up, Gilbert's breath caught…and his heart pounded!

Why was he so moved? What was this creature like that he had come so far and worked so hard to see? In his words:

> One flank was scored with a deep, partly healed, suppurating wound. It had lost an eye and was left with a socket of knotted, weeping scar tissue, which twisted its face hideously. It wheezed. Its jaws hung open. Its muzzle was covered with mucous, and its odor was rank.[39]

You see, he had no form or comeliness that we should look at him and no beauty that we should desire him. He was wounded for our transgressions; he was bruised for our iniquities. He was oppressed and he was afflicted, yet he opened not his mouth; like a lamb that is led to the slaughter, and like a sheep that before its shearers is dumb, so he opened not his mouth. Cat got your tongue, Jesus? Have you a soul? Can you reason? Can you talk? Nothing? Nothing? Very well, then let's see if you can suffer! And we took him out, and we slaughtered him…like an animal!

Like an animal. Is that not part of the point of this table? In spite of the condition of the Tassie devil that he saw, Gilbert said that it was a very satisfying animal, because it was "completely and convincingly another blood, known for a brief moment more intimately than I thought I would ever in my life know one of its kind."[40] I think that part of the magnetism that draws us to this table is not just the rite, not just the remembrance, but that persistent yearning we have for other bloods. The blood symbolized here is like ours, but somehow different. *This blood saves.* And here in these moments we know and experience that salvation more intimately than we deserve.

In the second century Melito of Sardis said that Jesus was born as a son, led out as a lamb, sacrificed as a sheep, buried as a man, and rose

---

[38]C. S. Lewis, in Bil Gilbert, "Nasty Little Devil," *Sports Illustrated* (5 October 1981), 76, 91.

[39]Gilbert, 91.

[40]*Ibid.*

from the dead as God.[41] What does it mean? It means that all things are connected. It means that Jesus Christ, the Alpha and the Omega, the first and the last, the beginning and the end, is also the Lord of the middle. And it means what God's middle children have known for aeons and we are only beginning to learn from people like Burt Mack—that we come to take life in the certainty that we will be taken.

Our hope is in that saving other blood of the one we follow, and whose good news we tell. Beyond the ashes, beyond the grave, there is new life for all of God's children. O Lamb of God, we come, too. Have mercy upon us, and bless the beasts and children. Amen.

---

[41]Melito of Sardis, *On the Passover*, tr. Richard C. White (Lexington, KY: Lexington Theological Seminary Library, 1976), 18.

123   TO CELEBRATE THE EMPTINESS

One of the joys of my life and work as a homiletician has been the emergence of significant female preachers. Trying to get a handle on the old head-versus-heart question, I have ungrammatically asked some of these splendid preachers "Where do you preach from?" And I have received a puzzling answer, as the women placed their hands on their midsection. One described it as "an empty spot deep within." Others spoke of "fear," "my own Carlsbad Cavern," "pain." One even smiled as she touched her stomach and said: "I call it 'my little green man.' He tears me up inside. But he also gives me my sermons."

I do not claim to be able to verify this, much less to understand it. But I do take it seriously, and realize that there are dimensions to the "source" of the sermon beyond scripture, tradition, reason, and revelation. And some of these dimensions are not yet grasped by many of us. The conclusion of Nelle Morton's essay on "Preaching the Word" contains the first example of what these women have been talking about that I have seen in print:

> ... the new woman can no longer buy the structured-from-above celebrative techniques. They come to her as manipulative and phony. With her sisters she knows celebration as out of the depths, out of the silent hollow darkness. Up from the roots. Thus we redeem the history of the word, looking to the Greek rather than to the Latin for its origins. *Cele* or *coele*, meaning "cavity, emptiness, hollow," with *brata*,

"to rule, command" becomes "to command the emptiness," to fill the void with that which by nature alone one does not possess.[42]

As I struggle to understand this in relation to the sermon, I wonder if the same principle applies to the Eucharist, not just for women, but for all of us. Martin Luther, preaching in 1522, said of the Eucharist:

> This food demands a hungering and longing man [quoting Augustine], for it delights to enter a hungry soul, which is constantly battling with its sins and eager to be rid of them. [Those] not thus prepared should abstain for a while from this sacrament, for this food will not enter a sated and full heart, and if it comes to such a heart, it is harmful.[43]

The picture becomes clearer. We do not commune out of our sufficiency but our need, not out of our satiety but our emptiness. Henry Nouwen tells a vivid story of a Zen master which parallels our concern:

> Nan-in, a Japanese master during the Meiji era (1868-1912) received a university professor who came to inquire about Zen. Nan-in served tea. He poured his visitor's cup full, and then kept pouring. The professor watched the overflow until he could no longer restrain himself. "It is overfull. No more will go in." "Like this cup," Nan-in said, "you are full of your opinions and speculations. How can I show you Zen unless you first empty your cup?"[44]

Nouwen goes on to say that in order to engender hospitality we must first create within a "friendly empty space."[45] It is this friendly empty space, this silent hollow darkness, that is the womb of Holy Communion. As Jesus "emptied himself, taking the form of a servant" for our sakes, so we come hungry to the table with empty "cups" that our lives might be filled anew with the spirit of Christ.

In the church where I worship, we hold the full cup as long as we want, drink when we want, and then hold the empty cup as long as we want. Holding the empty cup has become as important to me as holding the full one. Poured out. Given. Used up. Empty. Refillable. Celebrate that, too. It is the foundation of our faith. Only when we celebrate the emptiness, as our sisters have shown us, can we know the depths of God's love.

---

[42]Nelle Morton, "Preaching the Word," in *Sexist Religion and Women in the Church*, ed. Alice L. Hageman (New York: Association Press, 1974), 45.

[43]Martin Luther, "The Sixth Wittenburg Sermon," 94.

[44]*Zen Flesh, Zen Bones*, in Nouwen, *Reaching Out*, 54.

[45]Nouwen, 54.

124   THERE'S ROSEMARY

We all walked very slowly about the room, observing in silence, allowing that which we saw to do its work among us. Pieces from the AIDS Memorial Quilt were arranged in blocks on the floor. It was impossible to see and not be moved: "Jimmy, we love you." "John, we miss you so." I stopped before one of them. "There's rosemary. That's for remembrance. Pray, love, remember." That's what it said. Underneath were the words: "Shakespeare, *Hamlet*, Act IV, Scene 5." I wrote it down because I wanted to remember all manner of things from that day.

Returning home, I looked up the quotation and found it appropriately wreathed in sadness. Ophelia, struggling against madness, is seeking desperately to remember. There was clarity in the past, none in the present. Perhaps the person memorializing her or his loss of a loved one to AIDS is facing the same struggle. In fact, there are many gathered about the table on Sunday morning who are just barely hanging on. They have lost focus and hope and seek here something that will put them in touch with solid ground.

"On Christ, the solid rock I stand. All other ground is sinking sand." Perhaps this table can be of help in that regard. There's bread. There's wine. That's for remembrance. Pray, love, remember. Remember how much God loves you. Remember that Jesus loved you so much that he gave up everything for you. Remember that we gather around this table as a family of faith. We are for you, and you are not alone. If you are strong this morning, it is good that you are here, for there are people who need to lean upon your strength. If you are weak this morning, there are others here who are strong-shouldered today and happy to have you lean on them. As you need them, someday, in turn, they may need you. Remember that, too, and come all to the table of remembrance.

125   BARS AROUND THE TABLE

There are so many stories about this table: who may come, who may serve. Each of us no doubt has personal experience with exclusion or unexpected inclusion. I remember being invited to the table by a priest who served me at some risk to himself. I remember being in her home church with my sainted grandmother and seeing her denied communion because she was with me and the elders of that church did not like my theology.

Those who keep tight control over admittance to the Eucharist do so, I presume, because they believe this is a sacred feast that must not be profaned. And, up to a point, I can understand that (the point being Peter's vision in Acts 10: "What God has cleansed, do not call common.") Those who argue for open communion, as I do, do so simply because it is the Jesus' table and not ours.

Questions concerning who presides at the table follow similar arguments. Many churches do not permit women to officiate. This response by Frances Frank is the best I have ever seen and, to my mind, unanswerable:

Did the woman say,
When she held him for the first time
    in the dark dank of a stable,
After the pain and the bleeding
    and the crying,
        "This is my body;
        this is my blood."

Did the woman say,
When she held him for the last time
    in the dark rain on a hilltop,
After the pain and the bleeding
    and the dying,
        "This is my body;
        this is my blood."

Well that she said it to him then.
For dry old men,
Brocaded robes belying barrenness
    Ordain that she not say it
        for him now.[46]

Let us, all of us, come to the table now. Let us, all of us, serve one another in remembrance of him. Let us, all of us, work toward the day when there will be no more bars here designed to keep some people out, denied presence at the table, and to keep some people in, denied presence in the world.

---

[46]Frances Croake Frank, untitled poem in *Freeing Theology*, ed. Catherine Mowry LaCugna (San Francisco: Harper, 1993), 185-186. Used with permission.

126 THE FAT OF THE LAND

The first time I heard it, the phrase was applied to a crooked politician: "Ol' Dinky's just livin' off the fat of the land." The phrase "fat of the land" and its central word "fat" have come to have almost totally negative connotations. We do not like fat on meat or on ourselves. Recently the venerable Southwestern Exposition and Fat Stock Show had to change its name to "... Live Stock Show" because of the widespread aversion to fat. We spend billions on fad diets and many risk consequences of eating disorders like anorexia and bulimia—to keep from being fat. And we think of "fat cat" politicians as parasitic rather than creative.

All of this comes from our living in a fat-rich land. If we lived in a harsh place where the land was not so fat, we might look at it differently. A homesteader in northeastern Alaska, where one must "get your moose" before October or face serious consequences during the long winter, spoke of interior Alaska as a "fat-starved country," difficult for coastal people to understand.[47] Alaskans know that fat is a necessity of life, a storehouse for energy. They are thus closer to the classical—and biblical—understanding of fat, "the richest and most nourishing part of anything, the choicest produce of the earth."[48] Sometimes our lives seem barren, dry, poor, and empty. It may be worth considering that coming to the table in the midst of our need makes available to us not just grapes and wheat, but the fat of the land: the very finest and richest of earth's gifts—the symbols of our Savior's sacrifice. Low in calories, this feast still brings us the choicest portions: love, forgiveness, mercy, renewal, and hope. What a gift!

---

[47]John McPhee, *Coming into the Country* (New York: Bantam, 1979), 246.

[48]See definition 2.c., *Oxford English Dictionary*, vol. 4 (Oxford: Clarendon Press, 1961), 94.

127 THIS TABLE HAS WORK TO DO

In the Catskill Mountains back of Kingston, New York, is a road that winds along a hillside bordering an exquisitely lovely lake. Near a place where many stop to drink in the beauty of this scene with its cool breath of forest and sky is a sign: Ashokan Reservoir—New York City Water Supply. Your mind makes the journey of ninety miles to the south and you realize that the real business of this lake is not to provide anyone's private aesthetic enjoyment. It is to quench the thirst and clean the stain of a whole city.[49]

This story from Robert Luccock reminds us that even the beautiful has work to do. The service we perform about this table is for many a beautiful service: quiet, dignified, impressive. But that is not all it is. It has work to do. Its work is to sign for us week after week the new covenant we have with God through Jesus Christ.

Good point, I think. There is just one problem. Not long ago I read that the infrastructure for the New York City water system is breaking down. All the water for Manhattan and its millions of people comes through one pipe! And that pipe is old, rusted, broken in places, and leaking horribly. Maintenance has been deferred again and again for lack of funds, and the cost and logistics of replacement are astronomical. The whole system could break down at almost any time and leave the city without water. So while we are thinking about the work of this lovely table, we need also to remember that if we do not tend to the spiritual maintenance that gives this table its meaning, we risk a breakdown of the table's work. A beautiful table that does not work has limited value. A beautiful table that *cannot* work is a very sad thing indeed. Remember that.

---

[49]Robert Luccock, *If God Be for Us* (New York: Harper, 1954), 145.

128 ARSENIC AND OLD BREAD

In an old book of sectarian anti-Catholic sermons, there is a story about a priest who tries to persuade a young woman concerning the doctrine of transubstantiation, that the bread of the Eucharist is actually transformed into the very body of Christ. The young woman listens, then asks if she can bake the bread for Sunday's mass. It is agreed, and on Sunday, after the consecration and just before the distribution, the young woman stands up and asks the priest if the bread has now become the body of Christ. Assured that it has, she announces, "Then I assume that the spoonful of arsenic I put in the loaf has also been transformed." No one, including the priest, would eat.[50]

I assume the story is apocryphal, but I am old enough to remember the day when such a thing might well have been done to make a theological point. I do not mean to belittle those who stand firm for their theological convictions. Many have died in defense of various orthodoxies and heterodoxies. But I wonder if the debate about the substance of the loaf and cup might turn us from the more important consideration: that Christ died for us and that we now live in the grace and promise of that great sacrifice. I have come to the table all over the world. I have received good bread, bad bread, wafers, and those tiny chunks some churches favor. Whether or not they were actually the body of Christ, I do not know. But I ate them penitentially and gratefully in the glad knowledge that the Christ who died for us loves us still and remains as close to us as the air we breathe and the bread we eat.

---

[50]William Henry Book, *The Columbus Tabernacle Sermons* (Cincinnati: Standard Publishing, n.d.), 183-184.

129   GRABBING THE PAST

In one of my favorite *Doonesbury* cartoons, Mike and Zonker are walking down a Walden lane in a winter landscape. Zonker speaks:

> "That was quite a party last night, wasn't it, Mike? Another one for the memory books. I guess these really **are** the best times of our lives, huh, Mike? Bright college years! The midnight sledding parties, the study dates in the boat house, drunken drives to Boston....And the dean's Volvo! Remember parking it in the chapel? And getting busted at the Stones concert? And the time we all ran naked through the trustees' meeting!"

> "Uh...Zonker?"

> "Yes, Mike."

> "We never did any of those things."

> "I know, but one day we'll think we did."

> "Isn't it a little early to start embellishing?"

> "We're not getting any younger, Mike. You gotta grab the past while you can."[51]

---

[51]From a *Doonesbury* Sunday cartoon by Garry Trudeau, circa 1984.

Garry Trudeau has tapped into a human universal here. Life does not always happen the way we would like it, but our memories are very malleable. And if we recall a mind-made event long enough, we can begin to think it really happened. Put enough of these deceptions together and we lose touch with reality and begin to live in a fantasy world.

One of the blessings of sacramentality is the "stuff-ness" of it. Baptism requires water. Communion requires bread and wine. We may fantasize about the kind of Christ we would like to have, but bread and wine jerk us back to reality, to real love, and real suffering. Unlike Zonker, someday we will not think that perhaps God loves us—or was it a dream? We will gather again and again, break bread, drink from a cup, remember the truth, and know it for a fact.

Personal

PERSONAL

130 FRUIT AND CONSEQUENCES

One warm afternoon late in my fourth grade year, my little friends Ronnie, Mike, Don, and I were on the playground during recess. We were standing by the fence looking over into the back yard of the house that adjoined the playground when we noticed that the plum tree there was laden with fruit that was ripening. After a brief debate about fruit and consequences, we went over the fence, picked some juicy plums, and sat down giggling to enjoy the results of our adventure. Ronnie, Mike, and Don went right to work eating their plums, but I sat for a moment polishing mine in preparation for a real feast. It was then that we looked up and saw Mr. Wilson, who was about nine feet tall. Mr. Wilson yanked us all up and took us to the principal's office.

Our principal was named Noble T. Norman, which you must admit sounds like a principal's name. I remember that he made us wait for a couple of minutes standing there while he finished some work on his desk, an anxiety-heightening move on his part, which worked. He finally got up to face us.

"Ronnie, did you do it?" "Yes, sir."

"Mike?" "Yes, sir."

"Don?" "Yes, sir."

"Joey, did you do it?" "No, sir."

Noble T. looked hard at me: "Oh, you mean you didn't go over the fence and pick the fruit?"

"Well, sir, I did do that, but I didn't eat it." As far as I was concerned, if one did not enjoy the fruits of one's sins, then one was not guilty. Ronnie, Mike, and Don got two swats each with the "board of education." I got five. And, although I did not understand it at the time, Noble T. Norman gave me a real communion meditation that day: the point being is that you and I and everyone come guilty to this table, but we are no less guilty if we do not eat what is here. Not eating the bread of the covenant because we feel guilty makes us no less guilty. I agree with Paul that we should not profane the body and blood of the Lord by partaking of the elements casually and irresponsibly. But, burdened by sin, we are better off if we come to the table, confess that sin and receive these signs of grace and forgiveness, than we are if we stay away.

131 RESETTING A BODY OF BROKEN BONES

Eucharist can be a great puzzle. It is a breaking that can heal. I have heard many stories of angry enemies reconciled at the table. It is also a breaking which can exacerbate existing fractures. For example, one nineteenth-century American religious leader wrote that he had "resolved not to break the loaf with slaveholders or in any way to countenance them as Christians."[1]

From my own experience I remember the greatest ecumenical event I ever attended: the Quadrennial Student Conference held at Athens, Ohio, after Christmas in 1963. Thousands of students came from all over the world. There was a tremendous sense of energy and community, mission, and love. Coming to the table there was a profound experience. It was also one in which we ran into a stone wall. As the program booklet put it:

> Any ecumenical gathering is confronted with the brokenness of the Church in our time. To ignore the brokenness and cover it up by joining hands for a songfest does not deal constructively with the reality. We are broken, divided, separated....Therefore, three times during this week, several denominational services will be held at the same time.[2]

There is truth and sadness here. Not unlike the truth and sadness we encounter at this table. Winsome, blessed Jesus—crucified, mangled, broken. We might wonder: why celebrate such brokenness? Perhaps Thomas Merton puts it best:

> As long as we are on earth, the love that unites us will bring us suffering by our very contact with one another, because this love is the resetting of a Body of broken bones. Even saints cannot live with saints on this earth without some anguish, without some pain at the differences that come between them....Hatred recoils from the sacrifice and the sorrow that are the price of this resetting of bones. It refuses the pain of reunion.[3]

The sorrow we feel at the painful sacrifice of Jesus is real. But so must be our determination to be about the loving work of resetting the broken bones of the body of Christ. In doing so we find, strange but true, that our wholeness is to be found in our brokenness...and his.

---

[1]"Letter from Nat. Field, Jeffersonville," an 1834 letter cited by David Edwin Harrell, "The Sectional Pattern," *Discipliana* 21:1 (March 1961), 8.

[2]*Program Booklet for the 19th Ecumenical Student Conference on the Christian World Mission*, Athens, Ohio (27 Dec. 1963 – 2 Jan. 1964), 6.

[3]Thomas Merton, *New Seeds of Contemplation* (New York: New Direction Books, 1961), 72. This view of brokenness was first pointed out to me by Becky Hebert.

132   OLD, AND HUNGRY

Once, in Africa, I had a garden. An old donkey kept breaking in to eat my precious vegetables. I got more and more frustrated with him. Finally, I looked out one day, saw him in the garden, and lost my temper. I took a length of rubber hose and began beating him with it. I expected him to run away. What he did was collapse. Instantaneously, I saw what I had failed to see before, and my anger was replaced with guilt. He was an old donkey, no longer able to work, and thus worthless to his owner. So he had been cast out, abandoned, left to starve. One minute I had been beating him, the next found me sitting on the ground with his head in my lap and tears in my eyes, telling him not to die, that I would take care of him.

He survived; but that is not the end of the story. That day I divided my garden in half, led him in, and showed him: half was for him, half was for me. I thought I had done a noble thing. Some time later, I looked out a saw that he had broken into my half of the garden and was munching away. I ran out and shouted at him about his lack of gratitude. "I gave you half the garden! Wasn't that enough?" Then I learned my second lesson. As I led him back to his half, I looked and noticed that, while I had continued to water my portion, I had not done so to his, and his vegetables were brown and dying. You see, the decision to give a part of yourself, to commit yourself to another, is not enough. Even after you have given the garden away, you still have to water it.

There is a stewardship meditation there if you are interested, but the eucharistic images are also compelling. Think of those who have given their all, are used up and spent. Have you heard Carmen Bernos de Gasztold's beautiful "Prayer of the Old Horse"?

See, Lord,
my coat hangs in tatters,
like homespun, old, threadbare.
All that I had of zest,
all my strength,
I have given in hard work
and kept nothing back for myself.
Now
my poor head swings
to offer up all the loneliness of my heart.
Dear God,
stiff on my thickened legs
I stand here before You:
Your unprofitable servant.
Oh! of Your goodness
give me a gentle death.[4]

---

[4]Carmen Bernos de Gasztold, *Prayers from the Ark*, tr. Rumer Godden (New York:Viking, 1962), 61.

I could not help but think of "my" old donkey in reading these simple, touching words. What then is our responsibility to those who have given all they have to give? What is our responsibility to the man of Galilee who gave all he had that we might live, and does that responsibility transfer to those he died (and not gently) to save? What does it mean to remember him in this communion meal?

Think of the relationship between the offering and the communion. We give because God first gave. But God did not give once and never again. Neither can we. Even after we have given the garden away, even after we have dedicated ourselves to the way of Christ, we still have to water the garden, we still have to renew and refresh our spirits at this table of love and mercy. Talk the talk. Walk the walk.

133 LOREN'S COMING!

Years ago, when I was in seminary, the school fell upon hard times. We ran out of money. The cafeteria was closed, several beloved employees had to be laid off, all non-essential services were stopped. Two famous professors died, the Vietnam War was tearing the seminary community apart. In short, it was not the best of times.

And then some very strange things happened. An old professor stood up in chapel and made a startling suggestion. He suggested that it was time for us to do something really extravagant. In the midst of all the belt-tightening, cutbacks, and austerity, this shocked the community. But the more we thought about it, the more we decided he was right. And so the next week we threw a gala celebration, pulled out all the stops and had a wonderful party. To some who knew of the seminary's plight, it must have looked foolish, but to those of us who were there, it was an act of salvation.

I also remember Loren. He came to seminary, but found Protestant theology too insubstantial for his taste. So he left, took vows as a Dominican, and entered the monastery. He liked his plain and simple life as a Dominican, except for one thing. You see, Loren was a gourmet cook and there was no opportunity to practice this passion of his in the monastery. So three or four times a year he would take a day outside the cloister and the word would be passed down the hall: "Loren's coming!" We all chipped in what little money we had. Loren would go shopping and then disappear into the kitchen. We set up a big table in the hall and made the other preparations. Then we of the bologna-and-rice set would rejoice as Loren brought forth and described in almost spiritual language the succulent dishes he set before us. None of us will ever forget the extravagances of Loren's visits and his labors of love among us.

Many years ago there was a similar situation. Death was in the air. All that a group of people had worked for was about to come to naught. And then the leader who was about to be delivered up for execution began to do strange things. First there was a rowdy parade. Some wanted him to calm down his followers, but he said, "No, if they were to be quiet, even the rocks would shout." Let them celebrate. Then came a woman who poured an expensive jar of oil over his head. Some said the oil could have been sold with the proceeds going to the poor, but he said, "No, she is doing a beautiful thing." Then he threw a feast for his followers. And when it was done he gave them bread and wine to remember him by. This act of love, this act of extravagance in the midst of agony, calls us again and again to this table. Here we are reminded that his love for us is so extravagant that it knows no bounds, not even those of his own earthly life. So lay aside your burdens and come to the feast. There is none other like it in all the world. Good friends, Jesus is coming. Make ready.

134   THE MAN IN THE BLUE JACKET

When I was in graduate school in California, I rode my motorcycle several miles to school every morning. I soon noticed that at about 8:10 a.m., on a one-and-a-quarter mile stretch of open road between villages, I would meet a man riding a bicycle in the opposite direction. I waved, but he, tunneled into his riding, never waved back. In spite of that, seeing him each morning became important to me. I never learned his name or anything else about him, except that he rode a bicycle east on 6th Street out of Claremont at a few minutes past eight each morning, wearing, always, a blue jacket. But when I did not see him, I worried. Was he sick? Was there some problem in his family, if indeed he had a family?

Our regular "encounters" help provide a little structure in a disordered world. When I came over the rise by the orange groves and saw him peddling toward me, it was as if I was being reassured that the center holds, that "all's right with the world."

Receiving the Eucharist has been the occasion of some very intense experiences for me. But not every time. Sometimes it is just a quiet and warm experience as I recall that Christ loves us this much and everything is all right. I top the rise and see the man in the blue jacket and I smile. I take the bread and the cup and I see the Man for Others. I am glad that I know his name. I am even more glad that he knows your names. And mine.

135   TWO DANGERS IN SHARING OUR FAITH

Many years ago I travelled to and fell in love with a beautiful little village in Mexico named San Miguel de Allende. Later my wife and I visited the village again. And I have told others through the years about the village and urged that they go there. Recently a friend of mine did just that. We received a letter from him in which he said, "It is dangerous to recommend to another a place that has been important to you—because of the fear that he or she will not see it the same way you did." He did have a great time, but the sentence stayed with me.

As did this miserable experience. I stepped into a restaurant in New York and ordered shrimp. It was quite simply the best shrimp I had ever eaten. Large, luscious, melt-in-your-mouth shrimp. What a great experience! Some months later I was hosting a group of out-of-town guests. I remembered the restaurant and took them there, ordered shrimp for everyone, sat back with a smile and said, "Trust me." The shrimp came, and it was awful. Little pieces of shrimp from a package, cooked frozen, tough, tasteless. Great was my embarrassment. I later discovered that, in the interim between my visits, the ownership and cooks had changed, and the new specialty was surely not shrimp! It was still a good restaurant, but I should have let the people order for themselves.

Think about it. As we share the Christian faith, there is always the danger (or maybe the blessing, but that is another story) that others will not see it the same way we do. And that may be one reason that we come again and again to this table. Because the essence of our faith does not lie in particular propositions, but in the commonality of the love of Christ. We often say that this is not our table, and truly, it is not. It belongs to Christ. And it is spread for all, filled with many rich possibilities for understanding. It is not my place to order for you, to tell you what it must mean for you. My understanding may not be good for you. I believe that this table signifies the good news that Jesus Christ lived and died and lives again that we might all have life and have it more abundantly. That is the way I see it. But if you see it differently, you are no less welcome. Christ still invites you to come, eat, drink, and remember.

136   I DRINK IT AND I REMEMBER

I once had a student in California, a gentle Adventist named Bill Shelly. He was a splendid preacher. When Bill Shelly preached, angels flew in the window and danced. We used to talk a lot about things, Bill from his Adventist position, I from mine.

One day he told me a story about a camping trip he had taken with his wife, Edel. They drove to a beautiful place, pitched their tent, had a campfire, and went to bed. Bill woke up early, threw back the flap of the tent, and found himself face to face with a skunk.

The skunk let him have it, and Bill said it was awful. He had never been enveloped by such a powerful odor. He tried everything, bathed in the creek, even poured kerosene on himself, but nothing worked. Finally he remembered that his grandfather had told him that tomato juice was the cure. So they jumped in the car, Edel with a handkerchief over her nose and Bill driving with his head out the window so he could live with himself, until they got to a country store.

Edel rushed in. She came out in a couple of minutes and said, "They don't have any tomato juice. All they have is this," and she held up a can of V-8. By that time Bill wasn't particular. He took the V-8, ran into the woods, stripped off his clothes and rubbed the V-8 into his body: hair, face, everywhere. Then he washed off and, miracle of miracles, he was clean. He was "saved."

He went on to say that every once in a while, even now, he will be shopping in a grocery store, walking down the juice aisle, and he will see the V-8. He said, "I buy a can and take it home. And I drink it. And I remember."

For me Bill's story became more than just a story, because the eucharistic overtones are so powerful. And I took his story and used it in communion meditations across the country, grateful that a bad memory like a skunk, like Babylon, like a cross, could be the catalyst for new life. Good stuff, Bill. What promise you have as a preacher!

Then one day a postcard arrived. "Bill Shelly, former student at the School of Theology, was killed last weekend in a boating accident on Lake Havasu. His body has not been found. We knew that you had worked with Mr. Shelly and thought that you would like to know."

In my shock, I sat for a long, long time. Then I got up and went to a grocery store. I bought a can of V-8 and took it to a hill outside of town. I sat down. And I drank it. And I remembered.

137   RISKING COMMUNION

One day I was hiking on Shaw Island off the coast of Washington State. The day wore on and it was hot. I was thirsty and hungry. And just then I came upon a big beautiful berry bush. I picked a berry and, as I looked at it, I realized that I had never seen one quite like it before. It looked a little like a cross between a raspberry and a strawberry, but different, more delicate, a pale rose in color. I did not know what it was. It looked luscious…but could it be poisonous? So I just carried it around with me for the next several hours, taking it out of my pocket every so often to look at it and ponder, but afraid to eat it.

During my rambling that day it occurred to me that there would be nothing to eat in this world if somebody had not first taken the risk, tasted, survived, and told us that the food was good. Somebody had to show us that tomatoes were not poisonous (many thought they were) but that certain mushrooms were (many thought they were not). Somebody had to take the risk to let us know that apples are good food, while certain parts of the pufferfish are thirty times more deadly than strychnine.

The table spread before us today is laden with good food, symbols of the body and blood of Jesus. He took a risk, too. In fact, he risked everything, including his life, that we might have life. In trusting everything to God, Jesus risked oblivion. These elements before us are symbols of that great risk. We feast upon them in memory of him, in gratitude for the risk he took for us, and with the determination to risk being the people of God in our time. What is our risk in taking this bread and cup? Just that. That the message of the table might take, that we might leave this service different, changed, never to be the same again. Can we risk that?

By the way, it was a thimbleberry. And it was good.

138   TACTILITY

Jim Landes died this morning.[5] And we are in a state of shock. Only sixty-one years old. In the prime of his career. And apparently well. After the initial scurrying about to do what needs to be done, I sit down to think. Jim had the office next to mine, was a good friend, and had been a pallbearer at both my parents' funerals. And in thinking about Jim I remember the most poignant thing he ever told me.

Some years before, Jim had developed a medical problem. He went to a doctor who sent him to a cardiologist for a heart cath. The procedure was routine and Jim approached the whole thing with a sense of adventure. But it was not long before things turned frightening. A young cardiologist came into his room to announce that he had a 95% blockage of the LAD artery and that if it were not corrected, assuming that it could be, he was a 100% candidate for sudden death. Being a practical sort, Jim said, "Well, let's get it done." The P.T.C.A., as it is called, became a long ordeal. Jim watched from a cold table, the monitor above his head, as the physician worked and worked, trying to expand the small balloon he had maneuvered into the artery, while the surgical team waited across the hall, just in case. It seemed as though it were taking forever. Finally, Jim cried out, "Will someone, anyone, please come and touch me!" The loneliness, the coldness, the mechanical process going on gave him no assurance, no comfort, no counsel. Jim put it like this, "I felt a hand on my shoulder and it became for me the warmth of God. I could not see who it was that touched me and stood beside me for the rest of that procedure. I only know that in a moment I felt different. And I learned

---

[5] 25 Feb. 1994.

that day how even a stranger can manifest God's presence, can be God's touch, for another."

The saving grace for Jim was mediated that day through a real, but invisible, touch. And we have been made more gracious by Jim's touch. There is a real tactility to grace, one that we receive at this table as well. We hold the bread in our hands. We press the cup to our lips. This feast is not metaphysical. The bread and wine are real stuff. They remind us not only of sacrifice and atonement, but also of incarnation. God-with-us was real stuff, a human being named Jesus. He lived, he loved, he suffered. And there on the cross, in his greatest agony, there was no one to touch him. Those who loved him most could not reach out to him. What suffering that was.

And what wondrous love it is, then, that our cry, "Will somebody, anybody, please touch me," is often answered with the touch and taste of bread and wine. We talk about remembering Jesus with this service. But just as truly, we sing, "Jesus, remember me, when you come into your kingdom,"[6] and we *are* re/membered with a loving touch.

God bless and keep you, Jim. God bless and keep us all.

---

[6]"Jesus, Remember Me," chant from Taizé in *The United Methodist Hymnal*, 488.

139   EUCHARIST IS OUR LILAC

In the early 1980s I heard a lecture in California by South American theologian Rubem Alves.[7] Last month, rummaging through some files, I came across my notes of that lecture. If you are like me, notes you write tend to surface about once a decade. Anyway, at one point Alves said, "Eucharist is our lilac." I was impressed enough with what he said that I wrote it down and underlined it. Now, years later, I had a simple question: What in the world did he mean by that? Eucharist is what? A lilac? How? Why? The context in my notes was no help. It stood there by itself. What did it mean? The truth was: I had not a clue.

So, I thought about it. My knowledge of horticulture is minuscule. All I know about lilacs is that they are pretty and fragrant and perennial. I have never grown a lilac bush or lived where there was one. In fact, when I thought of lilacs, the first thing that came to my mind was not gardening, but poetry—specifically Walt Whitman's elegy for Lincoln. How did it go?

---

[7]Rubem Alves, "Theology of Body Poetry: Prophecy and Magic," Lecture at the School of Theology at Claremont, 8 Nov. 1983.

> When lilacs last in the dooryard bloom'd,
> And the great star early droop'd in the western sky in the night,
> I mourn'd, and yet shall mourn with ever-returning spring.[8]

So, in the spring of the preceding year, when the lilacs were in bloom, Lincoln had been assassinated. Whitman tells us that the fragrance and beauty of the blooming lilacs would, from that time on, remind him of Lincoln and his death. The connection had been indelibly made in Whitman's mind and would stay with him for the rest of his life.

Could that be what Alves meant? That the periodic partaking of the bread and cup will trigger in us the memory of Jesus as surely as the lilacs reminded Whitman of Lincoln? I like that, but we must step carefully here. The study of scripture drives toward recovery of the original meaning of the text, so that we can be as faithful to that meaning as possible in our interpretations. But just because we cannot always agree on what the biblical writers meant when writing, for example, about the Lord's Supper, we do not have to discard either the event or the text. Luke may or may not have had the Lord's Supper in mind when writing about Paul's breaking of the bread during the storm at sea. But believing that he did opens interpretative possibilities that can be very helpful to the faith community. And Acts 27:35 belongs now at least as much to us as it does to Luke or Paul.

So, when it comes to understanding the meaning of the Supper, I tend toward broader rather than narrower boundaries of understanding. I prefer a table without bars around it. Whatever else may have been on his mind, when he caught a whiff of lilacs, Whitman immediately remembered. And while I may not agree with the eucharistic theology of this or that group of folk, if I can smell Christ at the table, then it is a good place to be.

Someday I may see Alves again. If I do, I intend to ask him what he really meant by "Eucharist is our lilac." If I am wrong, I am willing to be set right. Till then, I will stay with this understanding. And I say to you: "Here we are at the table again, with words you may or may not like. But can you smell Christ here?"

---

[8]Walt Whitman, "When Lilacs Last in the Dooryard Bloom'd," reprinted in *Modern American Poetry*, ed. Louis Untermeyer (New York: Harcourt, Brace & World, 1958), 71.

140   MARANA THA!
1 Corinthians 16:21–24

I, Paul, write this greeting with my own hand. Let anyone be accursed
who has no love for the Lord. Marana tha! The grace of the Lord
Jesus be with you. My love be with all of you in Christ Jesus.

I sat down in the seafood restaurant. The young woman who came
to take my order was wearing a nametag. It said "Maranatha." I could
not help but comment, "You have an interesting name."

"It's a Bible name," she said.

"I know," I replied. "It means 'Our Lord, come!' or 'Come, Lord
Jesus.'"

"Yes," she exclaimed. "How did you know?"

"Well, I've been working on this word—or should I say your name—
for some time." She looked puzzled. "Marana tha," I went on, "is an
Aramaic phrase that found its way into the early Christian eucharistic
liturgy and into the New Testament (1 Corinthians16:22). When Christians gathered to break together, they would say at the opening of the
service, 'Marana tha!'"[9]

"And?"

"And I wonder. Does it mean 'Come, Lord Jesus, at the end of time'
or does it mean 'Come, Lord Jesus, right now in the midst of this communion and be with us'?[10]

"Could it mean both?"

"Yes, it could, and that's what makes it such an interesting name.
Not many people have time and eternity, now and forever, wrapped up
in their name."

The fish was good, but I may have been wrong. Every time we come
to the table, does not time meet eternity in the bread, does not now meet
forever in the cup, do not alpha and omega come together? Maybe that's
what makes "Christian" such an interesting name for all of us.

Marana tha!

---

[9]See Wainwright, *Eucharist and Eschatology*, 68-70.

[10]For an excursus on this possibility see D.M. Baillie, *Theology of the Sacraments*
(New York: Charles Scribner's Sons, 1957), 105. The contemporary Christian singing
group named Love Song uses this phrase effectively in their music.

Valedictory

VALEDICTORY

141 GALEED AND MIZPAH
Genesis 31:48–49

Laban said, "This heap is a witness between you and me today."
Therefore he called it Galeed, and the pillar Mizpah, for he said, "The
LORD watch between you and me, when we absent one from the other."

I make an end to this book with a story that has touched me. J. B.
Meharry (1845-1916) was an Irish Presbyterian pastor who served
churches in Ireland and England for over forty years. His last sermon
was preached at the communion service at Crouch Hill, London, on the
evening of September 26th, 1909:

> The church was crowded in every corner…, the attendance was the
> largest ever known in Crouch Hill. It had been decided by the Session
> that the final service should be sacramental. Dr. Meharry's meditation
> at the Communion was listened to with very earnest attention. It was a
> fit end to a remarkable ministry.[1]

What did Meharry say? Building on the covenant established between Jacob and Laban in Genesis 31, in which they set up a heap of
stones as a witness (*Galeed*) to their covenant and a pillar (*Mizpah*) as a
watchpost, praying that God would watch over them while they were
apart, Meharry piled up the stones of the congregation's common ministry: the Bible, the holy ordinances, the pastoral ministrations:

> We bring all these sacred stones together: memorials of a blessed
> past.…Upon what more fitting occasion could we do that than when
> we sit at this table, unworthy of the Lord's mercies yet keenly appre-
> ciative of the gifts of free grace, ushered by a mystic movement into
> the glorious spiritual life and adopted into a heavenly family.[2]

He then raised a pillar:

> The Lord watch between us! Time separates us; time hides one from
> the view of the other, but the Lord watches between.…Some will go
> away from this church tonight, from the Holy Supper, who will not sit
> here again. We part seemingly as minister and people. The Lord watch
> between us! As Jacob left that sacred stone, he met with angels. Could
> we make of this Holy Supper a blessed peace-time? I do not know. I
> know this: when we have raised our Galeed, our heap of witnesses,

---

[1]James Burns, "Memoir," *The Rev. J. B. Meharry, D.D.—Sermons* (London:
Hodder and Stoughton, 1917), 64-65.
[2]Meharry, *Sermons*, 225.

and when we have called the pillar Mizpah, saying, "The Lord watch between us," when we are passing one from another, we are on the way to meet angels.[3]

This is a moving scene, one in which the memorial meal of the church provides the setting for a congregation's own re/membering, and one in which the nostalgia and promise of Jesus, "I shall not drink it again until I drink it anew in My Father's kingdom," is experienced in the parting prayer of a beloved pastor: "The Lord watch between us." Meharry spiritualizes the supper, which is appropriate, though seldom done. The supper prompts a "mystic movement" which affirms our adoption into a "heavenly family." It is good to meditate upon the magnificent gift of God's free grace in Jesus Christ. And the daily grind of piling up stones is redeemed by the prayer, "Lord, watch," and the promise that God's angels are not far away.

---

[3]*Ibid.*, 231.